PELICAN BOOKS

THE COSTS OF
ECONOMIC GROWTH

Dr E. J. Mishan is Reader in Economics at the London School of Economics and has published a number of papers in professional journals. His other books include *Welfare Economics: Ten Introductory Essays* (1969), *Welfare Economics: An Assessment* (1969), and *Twenty-one Popular Economic Fallacies* (1969).

THE COSTS
OF ECONOMIC GROWTH

E. J. MISHAN

PENGUIN BOOKS

Penguin Books Ltd, Harmondsworth, Middlesex, England
Penguin Books Australia Ltd, Ringwood, Victoria, Australia

—

First published by Staples Press 1967
Published in Pelican Books 1969

—

Copyright © E. J. Mishan, 1967

—

Made and printed in Great Britain
by C. Nicholls & Company Ltd
Set in Monotype Times

TO RAY

Contents

Contents

Part Three

A Digression

More Intimate Reflections on the Unmeasurable Consequences of Economic Growth

Part Four

Preface

I

ABOUT the time of my appointment to the academic staff of the London School of Economics (November 1956) I had entered a pessimistic phase during which I was repeatedly afflicted with doubts about the value for human welfare of the growing tide of postwar economic expansion. That phase is not yet over. If anything my scepticism about economic growth has grown deeper with the years. The first published indication of my dissatisfaction with the fashionable view of economic growth as an obvious and desirable end of economic policy appeared in a review (*Economica*, May 1960) of a volume on the economics of underdevelopment edited by Agarwala & Singh. A month later The *Bankers'* *Magazine* (June 1960) published a short paper on 'The Meaning of Efficiency in Economics', which may be regarded as an embryo of the present essay. Off and on during the last few years I have continued to ponder about the connexions between welfare, industrialization, and technological advance and, occasionally, to discuss such themes informally with colleagues and students. However, it was only after Mr Arthur Seldon of the Institute of Economic Affairs suggested that my scepticism about economic growth might interest a wider public that I decided to make the attempt to bring my views together in a systematic manner, and to risk falling between two stools in addressing myself to the thoughtful citizen without making evasive simplifications. Thus, while I make no effort to conceal the general bias of my approach, wherever I have recourse to analytic argument I have sought to combine intelligibility with a level of sophistication that, though it may fail to satisfy some economists, is intended to be high enough to be of value at least to the undergraduate student of economics.

It is unnecessary to remark that my convictions about the ends of economic policy do not accord with popular preconceptions.

But neither do I imagine that I am quite alone in this respect. The skilled economist, immersed for the greater part of the day in pages of formulae and statistics, does occasionally glance at the world about him, and if perceptive, does occasionally feel a twinge of doubt about the relevance of his contribution. True, there is at the tip of his mind some faltering image of the blessings heaped on mankind as a result of rapid economic growth – a growing assortment of automobiles, television sets, vacuum cleaners, refrigerators, washing machines, electric tooth brushes and other anti-drudge devices, also increased education, increased air travel, antibiotics, and pesticides, and reduced infantile mortality. And yet, glancing at the irresistible spread of steel and concrete, at the plague of motorized traffic, at the growing impatience and tenseness of people, his thoughts may catch at a deeper apprehension of reality. For a moment, perhaps, he will dare to wonder whether it is really worth it; whether economic progress over the last couple of centuries has succeeded only in making life increasingly complex, frantic and wearing. The speed of travel grows from year to year, and from year to year more time is devoted in moving from one place to another. Physically, however, we are more idle and our lives more sedentary than our fathers. We know the world's business from minute to minute, and practically nothing of the people who live in our neighbourhood. Far removed from the forces of nature, denizens of the new subtopia, we are degenerating into a breed of passenger-spectators whose first impulse on awakening is to reach for a switch.

Like the rest of us, however, the economist must keep moving and since such misgivings about the overall value of economic growth cannot be formalized or numerically expressed, they are not permitted seriously to modify his practical recommendations. To be sure, various aspects of the social order are under continual attack by writers and intellectuals. But such attacks are expected in the normal course of events and, since such writers seldom have any claim to special economic knowledge, their strictures and dire predictions do not disturb the public unduly. Indeed the public has a remarkable faith in the ultimate beneficence of industrial progress, a faith which, it seems to think, could, in the last resort, be redeemed by modern economics. For this reason, a critique of economic growth by an economist may be taken more seriously. And certainly something will be gained if the public learns to appreciate the closeness of the links between rapid economic development and many of the unpleasanter features of our civilization. Once this is accomplished, the way is open to a general realization that there are more fundamental issues than just 'forward' or 'back'; that there are critical social choices yet to be debated if we can but turn our ears from the daily chanting of efficiency slogans reminiscent of 'Four legs good: two legs bad'.

II

Those who come to this volume after having read Professor Kenneth Galbraith's celebrated *Affluent Society* will observe some similarities. I certainly subscribe to his assertion that, in the face of changing economic circumstances, 'the conventional wisdom' – to use Galbraith's phrase – becomes increasingly irrelevant. None the less, it is worth making a distinction here between economic analysis proper and economic dogma. Whatever the value of economic analysis in its application to real problems, it lends no support to much of what we might call the folklore of economists. It is not possible, for instance, to make use of economic analysis to vindicate, with any pretence at generality, liberal presumptions in favour of freer trade, more competition, smaller public debt, or faster economic growth. Indeed such presumptions cannot be satisfactorily vindicated even by reference to fairly restricted premises about what matters. And if such presumptions continue to be held by a great number of economists, they are held purely on political grounds – though one suspects that their popularity among economists may be attributable in part to a close association, over the past two hundred years, between the development of economic theory and influential economic doctrines. A part also may be attributable to the typical construct by which economic theory advances, namely, the ideal system or model, having such initially simplifying features as perfectly competitive markets, perfect mobility of factors, perfectly free trade, perfect divisibility, which features themselves have in the fullness of time come to acquire normative overtones. Whatever be the explanation, however, Galbraith's conventional wisdom has reference to the presumptions or preconceptions of economists rather than to modern economic analysis.

This distinction assumes importance once it is recognized that economic presumption may be effectively undermined, and many popular propositions qualified, by recourse to economic analysis proper, especially that branch of it entering into the modern study of allocation problems. Thus, some part of Professor Galbraith's rejection of the economists' conventional preference for privately produced goods as against public goods might have been more formally expressed using the terminology of 'external diseconomies' explained in Part Two of this volume. And if, for his own purposes, Galbraith eschewed this concept in favour of a more direct and intuitive appeal, there are good reasons, notwithstanding, for elaborating the more formal arguments connected with this concept in the present volume. By inculcating more discriminating economic criteria in the public mind, the stock appeal to profits, exports, growth, or national interest may lose its efficacy, and people may come to expect discussions of economic policy to comprehend a far broader range of alternatives than those in the news today. In the second place, an understanding of the formal arguments will add authority to the representations of the many associations in this country committed to the thankless aims of protesting against noise, smoke, pollution and the destruction of wild life and natural beauty, that follow in the wake of expanding industry and communications.

If the reader notices the affinity of some of my conclusions in Part II with those reached by Professor Galbraith, he is also likely to notice some differences between us when he comes to read Part III. At the time of writing, at any rate, Galbraith appeared to be optimistic about the potential value of economic growth in an affluent society. No sign of any such optimism about the future will be found lurking in any corner of this essay – which is not to say, however, that very much cannot be done to make modern living a good deal more bearable than it is today.

III

The contents of this volume fall easily into its three parts. The first part contains a criticism of popular attitudes toward economic matters and the way in which such attitudes, passing for economic sagacity, impose severe political limitations on the opportunities facing a wealthy country such as Britain. Part II introduces the reader to the concept of external diseconomies, a concept crucial to any appreciation of the mounting spillover effects of modern industry and of its products on the amenity of society at large. The later chapters in that section are concerned chiefly with the broad principles on which the interests of society may be safeguarded and its range of choice extended. Part III hazards an incursion into those costs of industrial progress that do not lend themselves to formal analysis but are an essential part of the agenda in any inquiry concerning the social value of economic growth.

The three large digressions – on the balance of payments, on the transport problem, and on the unmeasurable consequences of economic growth – demand a word of explanation. A more finished work would, perhaps, have integrated them into the main structure of the thesis. Their matter is no less significant than that of the main text and, indeed, no less germane to the general theme concerning the social costs of economic growth. But in so polemical an essay it seemed desirable to focus the attention of the unspecialized reader on the most salient defect in the operation of our economy, though fortunately one within our power to remedy. By omitting the digressions on a first perusal the mind of the reader is likely to get the clearest impress of the main theme. And though it is my belief that the digressions reinforce the main theme, it is entirely possible for some readers to go along with the arguments in the text while having reservations about some of the digressions. The three appendices, on the other hand, add little to the volume. The first, on the possibility of technological unemployment, is obviously directed against the elementary fallacy that there can be no such animal. The other two are designed to convince economists of the validity of propositions appearing in the text and which may, at first sight, seem unfamiliar.

IV

For what may look like deficiencies in this volume, a word of explanation is owing to the reader. First, although I have made an attempt to disentangle some difficult issues that arise in any treatment of 'marginal cost pricing' and 'external effects', there is little in the analytic arguments of the chapters in Part II that would qualify as a contribution to knowledge. As already indicated, the aim of those chapters is, primarily, to popularize a certain method of thinking about economic problems which might serve to raise the level of public discussion. Second, as I shall remind the reader in the Foreword and in the Concluding Chapter, no attempt has been made in this essay to present a balanced picture of the social gains and losses arising from economic development in wealthy communities. I am concerned to disclose only some of the important connexions between economic development and social welfare, chiefly those that are imperfectly understood and frequently overlooked by the citizen. I have no inhibitions either about divulging my sense of dismay at what is happening about us, for the book is not offered as a work of scholarship, but rather as a tract for the times. These limited objectives serve to explain a third apparent deficiency, the impressive lack of documentation. There are almost no references to the professional journal literature, nor indeed to the more popular works on political economy ranging from Adam Smith's *Wealth of Nations* to postwar monographs such as Hayek's *Road to Serfdom* and Friedman's *Capitalism and Freedom*. In particular, in Part III, there are no references to many extremely relevant passages of Plato and to Sir Karl Popper's critique thereof in his *Open Society and Its Enemies*. In what I hope to be a popular essay in persuasion I wish to avoid any dissipation of the force of my arguments by scattering the pages with learned comments pointing to similarities and differences between my views and those of more celebrated authors. As for documentation of current instances of excessive social costs, in an exposition of principles the examples are chosen largely for the light they shed on the principles. And though it would have been possible to draw on some of the recent studies to illustrate the magnitudes of some limited spillover effects, such as river effluence, I attach far greater importance to promoting a public awareness of their nature and of the ways they ought to enter economic calculation.

On reading through the final draft I was not too surprised to discover that I was more repetitious than I had intended to be. But the points most frequently reiterated seemed worth reiterating in times such as these, and at the risk of subjecting the attentive reader to a modicum of tedium I decided to leave the text unaltered.

Finally, some readers may complain of a lack of detailed proposals or, worse, a lack of politically practicable proposals. But, at a time when the decencies of civilized living are daily beset by the exigencies of rapid material development, detailed proposals are secondary to what I deem to be the main task: that of convincing people of the need of radical change in our habitual ways of looking at economic events. As for political practicability, it is not too hard to foster a reputation for sound judgement and realism by a conspicuous display of moderation in moving with the times and a care to suggest nothing that the public is not just about ready to accept in any case. Such political sense has its uses, but it has nothing to contribute in any radical reassessment of social policy. Ideas that seem, at first, to be doomed to political impotence may strike root in the imagination of ordinary men and women, spreading and growing in strength until ready to emerge in political form. For what is politically feasible depends, in the last resort, on the active influences on public opinion.

v

I wish to acknowledge the courtesy of the editors of the *Journal of Transport Economics and Policy* for permission to reprint as Appendix C the greater part of my Note in the May 1966 issue of that journal. I wish also to acknowledge the courtesy of the editor of *British Industry*, Mr B. R. Russell, for his immediate response to my request to borrow some material from an article of mine which appeared in the March 1964 issue. Professor John Spraos of University College, London, was kind enough to read through the first draft of the digressions on the balance of payments and of the appendix thereon. I am indebted to him for drawing my attention to some loose ends in the arguments and for making suggestions that substantially improved the presentation. The generosity of three of my colleagues in permitting me to inflict on them various parts of the unfinished manuscript, during a period when the work of the School was making heavy demands on them, is gratefully recorded. Mr Laurence Harris and Dr Lionel Needleman gave freely of their time in discussing with me a variety of issues that arose in connexion with my first draft of Part III. Each of them pointed out blemishes in the original formulation. Dr Needleman, in addition to uncovering a number of stylistic infelicities, persuaded me to revise certain passages to distinct advantage. Mr Kurt Klappholz, with whom over the last ten years I have enjoyed countless discussions on problems concerning the relation between social welfare and economic policy, offered to read through the whole of the first draft, chapter by chapter. In the process of advising me at every turn in the arguments, he drew may attention to a host of defects in the arrangement and exposition. Though each of my colleagues is in broad sympathy with my views, I would not wish to implicate any of them in the details of my general thesis, nor in the remaining defects for which I alone am responsible.

October 1966   *E. J. M.*

Foreword

I

CONTRARY to their fashionable phrases about the need to face change, those who proclaim themselves to be in the vanguard of new thought prove to be in the iron clutch of economic dogma, much of it provided by famous economists of the past as a guide to policy in a world different from our own. Free trade, free competition, sustained economic growth, the free movement of peoples – these were, for Britain at least, the dominant economic aspirations of the nineteenth century. Nor were they entirely irrelevant after the turn of the century. Indeed, one might subscribe to such doctrines without self-deception until the close of the Second World War. For it was only after the first phase of the postwar recovery in Europe that one could descry the shape of things to come and, in that vision, doubt the relevance of these once-emancipating liberal doctrines to the momentous developments being wrought on our lives by the increasing pace of science and technology. The more salient among these developments are (1) the unprecedented expansion of the human species having ecological consequences we are only beginning to perceive, (2) the growing speed of technological advance and, as a corollary, the growing speed of obsolescence of skills, of knowledge and of culture, both esoteric and popular, and (3) the postwar surge of affluence in the West, much of it channelled into communications, in particular the mushroom growth of television, automobile ownership, air travel and mass tourism, phenomena that over a few short years have created a complex of urgent problems. Although the suddenness of these developments has caught us off our guard one might have thought that a modest concern with the welfare of society would have suggested the wisdom of setting aside inherited dogma and challenged us to think about what is taking place around us.

There may well be good explanations why this has not yet

17

happened. It is possible that our forms of government are better adapted to a more leisurely age, one in which social grievances could be redressed and problems met as they arose. Significant events, one felt assured, took time to shape themselves. Institutions need only change through the slow accumulation of knowledge and experience. As for the physical environment about us, it could be depended upon to hold its form for many years together. Thus men conditioned themselves to detect in the passage of events familiar patterns and parallels, and lulled their apprehensions whenever catastrophe appeared imminent with aphorisms about the illusion of change and about the basic sameness of the world in spite of appearances to the contrary.

Moreover, no provision is made, nor perhaps could it be made, for the sort of training that might fit a man to think about and judge of the effects on the welfare of ordinary people of a gathering eruption of science and technology in pressure sufficient to splinter the framework of our institutions and to erode the moral foundations on which they have been raised. In the course of his work a person of trained intelligence has little incentive to turn his mind to such tremendous questions. Whether working in the physical or the social sciences, those scholars who are not struggling abreast of the cumulating literature in their chosen field are struggling for recognition chiefly by attempting to publish original scientific work – an aim that is facilitated not by broadening but by narrowing yet further the focus of their enquiries. Economists are not excepted. Although many are interested in more than mathematical refinement and generalization for its own elegant sake, they do not tend to wonder aloud whether, for instance, the last two decades of material growth in the West has, on balance, further promoted the happiness of mankind. Such speculation, they might suppose, is better relegated to the amateur debating society. The world has more important matters to attend to. Such broad questions cannot, in any case, be systematically discussed using the purely technical apparatus of the social sciences; nor can they be discussed without the frequent invocation of 'value judgements'. And any social scientist who will dare to go so far in offending against custom and usage must be prepared to bear the withering scorn of those of the fraternity who have been more zealous in safeguarding their methodological chastity.

II

Whatever the explanation, we live in paradoxical circumstances. Notwithstanding the fact that bringing the Jerusalem of economic growth to England's green and pleasant land has so far conspicuously reduced both the greenness and the pleasantness, economic growth remains the most respectable catchword in the current political vocabulary. Even the younger men of today, struggling for the reins of power, habitually disregard, in their diagnoses of the times, the new sources of social conflict and social discontent emerging around us. They continue to give expression to the basic doctrines of their fathers and spin rhetoric out of the growth theme in blithe unconcern of the spreading jungle of problems stemming directly from the material prosperity of the last decade or so. They persist in minting phrases combining 'new' and 'change' and 'modern' and 'dynamic' as though these were cardinal virtues and in effect offer us all salvation by science – and via more exports. One factor that enables them to get away with their routine push-and-shove exhortation to the public is the postwar 'discovery' of that latest addition to the armoury of the Establishment, the economic index. A remarkably simple thing in itself, a mere number in fact, yet one that is treated with unabashed reverence. Apparently one has but to consult it to comprehend the entire condition of society. Among the faithful, and they are legion, any doubt that, say, a four per cent growth rate, as revealed by the index, is better for the nation than a three per cent growth rate is near-heresy; is tantamount to a doubt that four is greater than three. Such a doubt is not much worse than the doubt that economic growth itself, like the growth of knowledge, is not 'on balance' a good thing. Nonetheless, since many of the influences on our well-being (and possibly the major influences) – and in this essay we are to be concerned wholly with well-being, with welfare, satisfaction or happiness; possibly not measurable but certainly meaningful – do not lend themselves easily to the number system, it is not hard to show, as I propose to do in the following chapters, that doubts about a positive connexion between social welfare and the index of economic growth are amply justified.

Some of these influences, however, have not been entirely ignored by economists, though I shall suggest that the extent of their impact on social welfare has been grossly underestimated. The nature of these influences is indicated in the economist's standard critique of a perfectly competitive system whenever it is regarded as promoting an ideal allocation of resources. Since the turn of the century they have been systematically treated under the heading of external diseconomies. There are other criticisms, however, or misgivings at least, that go beyond those that may be comprehended by external diseconomies. These other criticisms do not depend for their validity and force upon the particular institutions by which a society allocates its growing resources and distributes its products. The economic growth of an affluent society under the direction of a highly centralized planning commission would be no less vulnerable to such criticisms than would be a decentralized and free enterprise system.

It would have been a pleasing intellectual exercise to have formalized these latter criticisms, if only to contain them within the field of economics and thereby to strengthen their appeal to my colleagues. But it cannot really be done. The economist who is sympathetic to my views may have to accept many arguments that cannot be tucked comfortably into some corner of any structure of welfare economics.

III

What I wish to be concluded from this essay might usefully be summarized here: that the popular postwar dichotomy drawn between the 'establishment' on the one hand and the 'progressives' on the other – or, to vary the terminology, between the traditionalists and the old school on the one hand and the 'modernizers' and 'pacemakers' on the other – has served to confuse the chief issue that confronts us: that of seeking to adjust the environment to gratify man's nature or of adjusting man's nature to an environment determined predominantly by 'efficiency considerations', that is, by technological advance.

One could, of course, decide to use words differently and, therefore, to agree that the issue is that between 'facing change' and 'going on in the same old way', provided that we dissociate 'facing change' from the inertia of mere momentum and, more specifically, from the orthodox measures that invariably feature on the agenda of our would-be 'pacesetters' – increasing competition, pushing exports, increased technological efficiency and, above all of course, faster economic growth. For those who, from habit as much as conviction, hanker after these things, who are impatient to hustle us into the future, painful though it may be, are not, on an alternative use of language, facing the twentieth century at all. They are merely trimming their sails to the winds of fashion. The phrase 'facing the twentieth century' might better refer to the need, in the face of a new and incalculable power of the rising technology, to surrender the simple faith in the beneficence of industrial progress guided only by ancient presumption in favour of liberal economic doctrines. Stated more positively, the younger generation will be facing the future with honesty only when it brings itself to face the strain of thinking through the consequences, tangible and intangible, certain and speculative, of the current drift into the future and, in doing so, recognizes that in the new world the old liberal economic harmonies are not to be found; that on many issues painful choices have to be made, and that in some cases the needs of men and the needs of technology may prove to be irreconcilable.

I am far from being unaware that many of my arguments will not stand up to so-called scientific scrutiny; that many assertions are made without the attempt to present evidence. For this I hold the present state of knowledge to be at fault, not my arguments. Owing to the speed with which events have overtaken our analytic and statistical techniques we have not yet evolved methods for estimating the more outstanding external diseconomies of the postwar era. Yet such is our perverse faith in figures that what cannot be quantified is all too often left out of the calculus altogether. There is apparently a strong prejudice among research workers against admitting that the unmeasurable effects are likely to be more significant than the measurable ones, and that in such cases, therefore, any conclusions reached on the basis of the measurable effects only are unwarranted.

Be that as it may, since there does not appear much likelihood of our being able to estimate these growing diseconomies, or 'social costs' as they are sometimes called, in the near future it is more urgent that they be brought to the attention of the public in the most graphic manner rather than have writers relegate them to apologetic footnotes. The undeniable fact that no estimates have been made, or are likely to be made shortly, about the magnitude of some untoward social effect need not intimidate the economist from occasionally respecting the plain and inescapable evidence of his own senses. Nor should such a fact prohibit his reasonable conjectures about the future if present trends remain unchecked.

As for those consequences of rapid technological advance that do not, even in principle, lend themselves easily to measurement, one cannot await the advent of a more accommodating methodology before considering them in earnest, since they seem yet more portentous than those which are measurable in principle. Here, the appeal to the reader in the final section – 'The Unmeasurable Consequences of Economic Growth' – must of necessity be in terms of familiar experience and intuitive knowledge. I make no claim, however, to have presented a balanced picture. Since there is no danger of the alleged benefits of economic growth being understated by the scientists and technocrats who today have the public ear, prior to taking over the earth tomorrow, one may safely assume that the glowing tints in the picture have not been toned down. I can apply myself without compunction, therefore, to daubing in the black spots.

I shall not pretend that the task has been uncongenial, and there may well be places where the flow of ideas and of feeling has carried the argument beyond a point that can be comfortably sustained by reason alone. On the whole, however, I think the incursion into this only faintly charted territory has been worth while, if only for the opportunity it afforded of giving systematic expression to my own misgivings about the world which technology is shaping for us. But I also entertain the hope that, on putting the book down, some sympathetic reader will contemplate the future with more concern, or less complacency, than when he took it up.

Part One

1

Growthmania

REVOLUTIONS from below break out not when material circumstances are oppressive but, according to a popular historical generalization, when they are improving and hope of a better life is in the air. So long as toil and hardship was the rule for the mass of people over countless centuries, so long as economic activity was viewed as a daily struggle against the niggardliness of nature, men were resigned to eke out a living by the sweat of their brows untroubled by visions of ease and plenty. And although economic growth was not unheard of before this century – certainly the eighteenth-century economists had a lively awareness of the opportunities for economic expansion, through innovation, through trade and through the division of labour – it was not until the recent postwar recovery turned into a period of sustained economic advance for the West, and the latest products of technological innovation were everywhere visible, and audible, that countries rich and poor became aware of a new phenomenon in the calendar of events, since watched everywhere with intentness and anxiety, the growth index.[1] While his father thought himself fortunate to be decently employed, the European worker today expresses resentment if his attention is drawn to any lag of his earnings behind those of other occupations. If, before the war, the nation was thankful for a prosperous year, today we are urged to chafe and fret on discovering that other nations have done perhaps better yet.

Indeed with the establishment of the National Economic Development Council in 1962 economic growth has become an official feature of the Establishment. To be *with* growth is

1. Like a national flag and a national airline, a national plan for economic growth is deemed an essential item in the paraphernalia of every new nation state.

manifestly to be 'with it' and, like speed itself, the faster the better. And if NEDC, or 'Neddy' as it is affectionately called, is to be superseded, it will be only to make way for larger and more forceful neddies. In the meantime every businessman, politician, city editor or writer impatient to acquire a reputation for economic sagacity and no-nonsense realism is busy shouting giddy-up in several of two-score different ways. If the country was ever uncertain of the ends it should pursue, that day has passed. There may be doubts among philosophers and heart-searching among poets, but to the multitude the kingdom of God is to be realized here, and now, on this earth; and it is to be realized via technological innovation, and at an exponential rate. Its universal appeal exceeds that of the brotherhood of man, indeed it comprehends it. For as we become richer, surely we shall remedy all social evils; heal the sick, comfort the aged and exhilarate the young. One has only to think with sublime credulity of the opportunities to be opened to us by the harvest of increasing wealth: universal adult education, free art and entertainment, frequent visits to the moon, a domesticated robot in every home and, therefore, woman forever freed from drudgery; for the common man, a lifetime of leisure to pursue culture and pleasure (or, rather, to absorb them from the TV screen); for the scientists, ample funds to devise increasingly powerful and ingenious computers so that we may have yet more time for culture and pleasure and scientific discovery.

Here, then, is the panacea to be held with a fervour, indeed with a piety, that silences thought. What conceivable alternative could there be to economic growth? Explicit references to it are hardly necessary. When the Prime Minister talks with exaltation of a 'sense of national purpose' it goes without saying that he is inspired by a vision, a cornucopia of burgeoning indices.

But to be tediously logical about it, there is an alternative to the post-war growth-rush as an overriding objective of economic policy: the simple alternative, that is, of not rushing for growth. The alternative is intended to be taken seriously. One may concede the importance of economic growth in an indigent society, in a country with an outsize population wherein the mass of people struggle for bare subsistence. But despite ministerial twaddle about the efforts we must make to 'survive in a competitive world', Britain is just not that sort of country. Irrespective of its 'disappointing' rate of growth, or the present position of the gold reserves it may be reasonably regarded, in view of its productive capacity and skills, as one of the more affluent societies of the West, a country with a wide margin of choice in its policy objectives. And it is palpably absurd to continue talking, and acting, as if our survival – or our 'economic health' – depended upon that extra one or two per cent growth. At the risk of offending financial journalists and other fastidious scrutinizers of economic statistics, whose spirits have been trained to soar or sink on detecting a half per cent swing in any index, I must voice the view that the near-exclusive concern with industrial growth is, in the present condition of Britain, unimaginative and unworthy.

The reader, however, may be more inclined to concede this point and to ponder on a more discriminating criterion of economic policy if he is reminded of some of the less laudable consequences of economic growth over the last twenty years.

Undergraduate economists learn in their first year that the private enterprise system is a marvellous mechanism. By their third year, it is to be hoped, they have come to learn also that there is a great deal it cannot do, and much that it does very badly. For today's generation in particular, it is a fact of experience that within the span of a few years the unlimited marketing of new technological products can result in a cumulative reduction of the pleasure once freely enjoyed by the citizen. If there is one clear policy alternative to pressing on regardless, it is the policy of seeking immediate remedies against the rapid spread of disamenities that now beset the daily lives of ordinary people. More positively, there is the alternative policy of transferring resources from industrial production to the more urgent task of transforming the physical environment in which we live into something less fit for machines, perhaps, but more fit for human beings.

Since I shall illustrate particular abuses of unchecked commercialism in later chapters and criticize them on grounds familiar to economists, I refrain from elaboration at this point. However, it is impossible not to dwell for a moment on the most notorious by-product of industrialization the world has ever known: the appalling traffic congestion in our towns, cities and suburbs. It is at this phenomenon that our political leaders should look for a really outstanding example of postwar growth. One consequence is that the pleasures of strolling along the streets of a city are more of a memory than a current pastime. Lorries, motor-cycles and taxis belching fumes, filth and stench, snarling engines and unabating visual disturbance have compounded to make movement through the city an ordeal for the pedestrian at the same time as the mutual strangulation of the traffic makes it a purgatory for motorists. The formula of mend-and-make-do followed by successive transport ministers is culminating in a maze of one-way streets, peppered with parking meters, with massive signs, detours, and weirdly shaped junctions and circuses across which traffic pours from several directions, while penned-in pedestrians jostle each other along narrow pavements. Towns and cities have been rapidly transmogrified into roaring workshops, the authorities watching anxiously as the traffic builds up with no policy other than that of spreading the rash of parking meters to discourage the traffic on the one hand, and, on the other, to accommodate it by road-widening, tunnelling, bridging and patching up here and there; perverting every principle of amenity a city can offer in the attempt to force through it the growing traffic. This 'policy' – apparently justified by reckoning as social benefits any increase in the volume of traffic and any increase in its average speed – would, if it were pursued more ruthlessly, result inevitably in a Los Angeles-type solution in which the greater part of the metropolis is converted to road space; in effect a city buried under roads and freeways. The once-mooted alternative, a Buchanan-type plan – 'traffic architecture' based on the principle of multi-level separating of motorized traffic and pedestrians – may be an improvement compared with the present drift into chaos, but it would take decades to implement, would cost the earth, and would apparently remove us from contact with it. The more radical solution of prohibiting private traffic from town and city centres, resorts and places of recreation can be confidently expected to meet with the organized hostility of the motoring interests and 'friends of freedom'. Yet, short of dismembering our towns and cities, there is no feasible alternative to increasing constraints on the freedom of private vehicles.

II

Other disagreeable features may be mentioned in passing, many of them the result either of wide-eyed enterprise or of myopic municipalities, such as the postwar 'development' blight, the erosion of the countryside, the 'uglification' of coastal towns, the pollution of the air[2] and of rivers with chemical wastes, the accumulation of thick oils on our coastal waters, the sewage poisoning our beaches, the destruction of wild life by indiscriminate use of pesticides, the change-over from animal farming to animal factories, and, visible to all who have eyes to see, a rich heritage of natural beauty being wantonly and systematically destroyed – a heritage that cannot be restored in our lifetime.

To preserve what little is left will require major legislation and strong powers of enforcement. But one cannot hope for these without a complete break with the parochial school of economics that has paralysed the mind of all governing authorities since the industrial revolution. It will require a new vision of the purposes of life to stand up to the inevitable protests of commerce, of industry, and of the financial journalists, protests that employment, expansion, exports – key words in the vocabulary of the parochial school – will be jeopardized if enterprise is not permitted to develop where profits are highest.

Our political leaders, all of them, have visited the United States, and all of them seem to have learned the wrong things.

2. According to Professor L. J. Battan, of Arizona, *The Unclean Sky: A Meteorologist looks at Air Pollution*, the air above is treated as a vast sewer. Gases have been poured into the atmosphere in the mistaken belief that the wind, like a river, would not only carry the wastes away but somehow purify them in the process. As a result, some ten million tons of solid pollutants are now floating around in the sky. There is, however, a limit to what the finite atmosphere can safely disperse: what goes up must eventually come down.

They have been impressed by the efficient organization of industry, the high productivity, the extent of automation, and the new one-plane, two-yacht, three-car, four-television-set family. The spreading suburban wilderness, the near traffic paralysis, the mixture of pandemonium and desolation in the cities, a sense of spiritual despair scarcely concealed by the frantic pace of life – such phenomena, not being readily quantifiable, and having no discernible impact on the gold reserves, are obviously not regarded as agenda.

Indeed, the jockeying among party leaders for recognition as the agents of modernization, of the new, the bigger and better, is one of the sadder facts of the postwar world, in particular as their claim to the title rests almost wholly on a propensity to keep their eyes glued to the speedometer without regard to the direction taken. Our environment is sinking fast into a welter of disamenities, yet the most vocal part of the community cannot raise their eyes from the trade figures to remark the painful event. Too many of us try not to notice it, or if occasionally we feel sick or exasperated we tend to shrug in resignation. We hear a lot about the 'cost of progress', and since the productivity figures over the years tend to rise we assume that on balance, and in some sense, we must be better off.

III

In the endeavour to arrest this mass flight from reality into statistics, I hope to persuade the reader that the chief sources of social welfare are not to be found in economic growth *per se*, but in a far more selective form of development which must include a radical reshaping of our physical environment with the needs of pleasant living, and not the needs of traffic or industry, foremost in mind. Indeed, in the later chapters I shall argue that the social process by which technological advance is accommodated is, in any case, almost certain to reduce our sources of gratification in life. Before launching into these main themes, however, something must be said about two things: (1) that myth which persuades us that, as a nation, we have no real choice; that living in the twentieth century, we are compelled to do all sorts of things we might otherwise not wish to do, and (2) Britain's foreign trade, as a particular instance of the no-choice myth. Since childhood, all too many of us have lived in awe of the balance of payments, and now that growth is all the rage, indeed an imperative, we have unthinkingly come to link faster growth with an improved balance of payments. We ought, first therefore, to examine briefly the much misunderstood relation between economic growth and the balance of payments, after which we should reconsider a traditional belief in the importance of a large volume of foreign trade.

Enough will be said, I hope, to indicate that there is a great deal more choice in matters of foreign trade than is usually conveyed by the newspapers, at least enough to free us from the imagined compulsion of having to expand rapidly, and from popular fears of 'not surviving', or 'being left behind in the race', or 'stagnating in an amiable backwater', *ad nauseam*. Having pushed aside such matters, we are free to extend the rationale of the market mechanism in order to explain how the persistence of commercial habits of thought is responsible for the creation of so much 'diswelfare'. We may then move on to consider the principles that should inform the policies of any government that is at all concerned with the well-being of ordinary people.

2

The No-choice Myth

LET us begin by being platitudinous to the point of remarking that all three possible goals of long-term policy – (1) economic growth, (2) a more equitable distribution of the national product, and (3) improved allocation of our national resources – play some part in the complex of existing economic policy. Differences of opinion may therefore be attributed to differences in emphasis. For many years now the emphasis has been almost entirely on growth, whereas one of the themes of this essay is that it ought to be almost entirely on improving the allocation of our existing resources. It is the task of these first chapters to persuade the reader of the urgent need for this shift in priorities.

Before inspecting these long-term goals more closely, let us distinguish them from the perennial concerns of the day-to-day running of the country which too often appear wholly to absorb the energies of the government. These routine preoccupations, which go to fill the financial columns of our newspapers and are the subject of inumerable reports, are three in number: (a) the maintenance of a high level of employment, (b) the stabilization of the level of prices, and (c) the promotion of a favourable balance of payments. In so far as we succeed in these objectives we refer to the economy as 'healthy' or, better yet, 'sound'. Certainly it would be reckless to ignore the indices of the current performance of the economy. Any time that (a) a large proportion of the voluntary labour force is without employment, or (b) an initially suppressed inflation has slipped its restraints and a distrust of the currency is spreading, or (c) there is no reasonable prospect of paying for the inflow of goods from abroad, a sense of crisis impends and there is warrant enough for temporarily overlooking long-term goals in the immediate attempt to return the economy to a more acceptable norm in any of these respects. The economy may be likened to an engine whose smooth functioning is indicated by governors labelled 'employment', 'price stability' and 'balance of payments'. Obviously any poor performance calls for repairs; and it is the task of a good mechanic to avoid breakdowns and ensure the good condition of the engine. But keeping the engine trouble-free is not an end in itself. The engine drives a vehicle, and the speed of the vehicle to some extent, and the direction it takes, to a greater extent – long-term policies – are what really matter.

Since national self-castigation, in all economic matters at least, has been in high fashion since the war, one must risk the charge of unpardonable complacency by the reflection that our postwar record has been good enough compared with those of other countries. We have enjoyed a very high level of employment (some economists would say too high), and though in consequence prices have indeed risen they have not risen at a dangerous speed. The balance of payments position, though frequently troublesome, is not intractable and may be resolved by a variety of measures none of which is likely to cause any great hardship. Our growth rates, as we all know, appear near the bottom of the international league table. But if we can bear to live with this mortifying fact,[1] we can still live comfortably. None the less, the attention paid to these popular indicators of 'economic health' is excessive when compared with any critical analysis of our long-term plans. An explanation of the popularity of this sort of 'index economics', especially among financial journalists, may well be that an aptitude for summarizing official figures, for the uttering of grave warnings whenever there is a down-turn in the graphs, is not a difficult one to pick up.

The knowledge that several hundred financial journalists and government officials pursue this hobby – tabulate figures (to the

1. Not every kind of growth index, however, would place Britain near the bottom of the list. Much would depend upon the base period adopted, the length of the period chosen, the goods included and their relative weights in the index. If frequent tea-breaks and other manifestations of disguised leisure are regarded as *goods* – and economics suggests they be so regarded – their conceivable quantification and inclusion in any index of output *per capita* might go some way to enhance Britain's comparative performance.

nearest million), construct charts, and spin endless columns of verbal statistics – is something we might continue to put up with were it not for the fact that the fascination with index economics detracts attention from the broader aims of economic policy, and tends to become a substitute for them. We become so preoccupied with the ups and downs of the indices that we fail to raise our sights to the larger issues that confront us. Continuously arguing about and tinkering with the economic engine, we have only afterthoughts to spare for the rapid and visible changes taking place about us. In the event, there is no general awareness by the public of the range of significant social choices facing it.

Admittedly the economic engine has not been turning very smoothly for some time, but the trouble is, in the last resort, more political than economic.

In a bid to capture public support successive governments have gone out of their way, over the last fifteen years, to implant expectations of rising incomes and opportunities. More recently, official support of arbitrary growth targets has as much as invited annual wage-claims by the trade unions. Having so assiduously sown the seeds of rising expectations we are reaping the harvest of rising prices. A slow but uninterrupted inflation over the last quarter of a century has imparted to the economy a psychological momentum: workers, managers, bankers, professional men, shareholders, all anticipate rising incomes and prices to continue over the future notwithstanding anything governments may do.

The political commitment to a fixed parity for sterling and to support for a level of employment that is evidently well within the inflationary zone, however, makes it risky for governments to do the obvious things – introduce effective flexibility into the price of sterling and into monetary policy. They have turned, instead with singular lack of success, to increased reliance on fancy fiscal measures, to dramatic announcements of changes in Bank rate, and to brave but ineffectual ministerial speeches exhorting us to work harder and export more, all of which give greater impetus to the preoccupation with index economics and to dilettantism among financial journalists.

I cannot see this country in the near future freeing itself from the exhausting preoccupation with the internal and external value of its currency, and from drifting from one petty crisis to another – and, therefore, among the endless bickering and hullabaloo, neglecting the growing disamenities about us and the consequent urgency of revising our long-term economic policy to deal with them – (1) unless the Government is ready to make more frequent and more drastic changes in the money supply, and to accustom businessmen to respond without consternation to wider and more frequent movements in Bank rate and security prices;[2] (2) unless the Government is prepared to see the employment figure decline below the 98 per cent level;[3] and (3) unless the government is prepared to promote flexibility in the price of sterling to enable us to determine our domestic policy, primarily and for all times, by reference to the domestic situation and not, as at present, primarily by reference to the state of our foreign exchange reserves.

2. There is one non-political argument against the vigorous use of monetary policy – a policy that entails more frequent and more drastic (though less dramatic) changes in Bank rate and also in the supply of money – vigorous enough to exert the required pressure notwithstanding the high liquidity of the private sector: the instability argument. If monetary policy is used as timidly as it is currently being used, then it will continue to be ineffective. If, on the other hand, the measures taken are drastic enough to be effective they will, it is suggested, be too effective, i.e. once the pressure begins to tell it will send the economy into a downward spin. The strong measures required to correct this downward movement will, in their turn, 'overshoot the mark' and send the economy soaring into inflation.

If this were a fact of economic life we might well despair of deflecting the economy from the path of perpetual inflation. But though it is a common view, and one that lends support to those who would avoid politically un-popular measures, there is just no evidence to support it. Indeed, in an economy in which changes in Bank rate and in the money supply are infre-quent and limited, the data necessary for testing this peculiar instability hypothesis do not exist. In these frustrating circumstances there is much to be said for bolder experiments with monetary measures.

3. We may have to learn to live with the unpalatable social fact that (at least in a non-totalitarian society) price stability requires x per cent unem-ployment on the average, where x is greater than two. This may not be un-bearable if the turnover of the unemployed pool is fairly rapid and, also, if substantial increases in unemployment pay come into force.

It does not seem self-evident to me that if the need for these measures were put fairly to the public they would be rejected. But even if they were received, initially, with ill grace, they should – at least if we believe in their efficacy – be brought continuously to the attention of the public. In view of this desideratum it is discouraging, though perhaps not surprising, to observe that whenever the economist gets too close to the machinery of government he is all too prone to talk the language of 'political feasibility'. In order to avoid frustration he may learn to advocate only those measures he believes stand some chance of acceptance. This implies, however, failure to advocate technically efficient measures for fear of being ignored by governments whose range of policies is limited by party ideology, financial shibboleths and public prejudice. But once the economist succumbs to the easy habit of making only those recommendations that accord with 'political realities' he soons finds himself in the uncomfortable position of using his authority to sanction the political fashions of the day.

II

There is, however, one more reason why we have failed to take the straightforward measures referred to, preferring instead to tinker with a ragbag of fiscal devices, and this is the popular belief that faster growth is the real solution to our chronic economic infirmities. If only we can 'get Britain moving', presumably at the official $3\frac{1}{2}$ per cent growth rate, inflation would cease to plague us and our balance of payments problems would cease. Indeed, there is a two-way connexion here: if faster economic growth is believed by some to enable us to overcome the problems posed by excess imports and rising prices, the same people are also apt to believe that success in increasing exports and stabilizing prices improves the prospects for economic growth. Thus, if we are all of us opposed to 'stop-go' policies, it is not because the excitement is too much for us, not even because they cause great hardship in themselves, but because these periodic reversals of monetary and fiscal measures taken by successive governments are believed to be detrimental to sustained economic growth. If we worry about creeping inflation, it is not so much because of its inequitable distributional effects as for fear of losing exports. And, as indicated, there are many who believe that increased exports is both a pre-condition and an effect of increased economic growth.

This is the circle of reasoning within which we have been confined during the last decade or so and which is predominant in official quarters. It is a circle of reasoning that seems to leave us little choice. We appear to be caught in a treadmill, wherein we must press harder if we are to 'keep up in the race', or even to survive. Yet, if the truth must be told, there is no economic warrant for such constricting beliefs. We have only ourselves to blame if our no-nonsense patriots have mesmerized us over the years into this unrelenting frame of mind.

With the rapid growth in the popular channels of communication it is more true than ever before that the sheer weight of reiteration rather than the power of reason influences the attitude of the public. A simple term such as 'growth potential' is loaded with compulsion: it suggests that waste is incurred whenever we fail, as invariably we do, to realize this potential growth. It is a term apt to the technocratic view of things, that envisages the country as some sort of vast power-house with every grown man and woman a potential unit of input to be harnessed to a generating system from which flows this vital stuff called industrial output. And since this stuff can be measured statistically as GNP (Gross National Product), it follows that the more of it the better. Viewed as power-houses for producing GNP certain countries appear to perform better than Britain. It is obvious, therefore, that we must make every endeavour to catch up. Moreover, other countries use more engineers and more PhDs per million of population than we do. Also they have a higher productivity. It follows that we *need x* per cent more engineers and *y* per cent more PhDs. To continue, steel output could, if we tried hard, rise to *z* million tons by 1970, as much *per capita* as the US has now. In consequence, we *need* to expand steel capacity at *w* per cent per annum. Again, in order for every family in Britain to have its own motor-car by 1975 we need to expand the motor-car industry at v per cent per annum. With such 'needs of industry' to be met we shall require increased commercial transport and, therefore, increased imports of fuel. Consequently we *need* to work harder in order to pay for our *needs*. And so we go on, slipping from implicit choices to explicit imperatives.

It would be futile, of course, to suggest that we should be thinking about the possibilities of reducing the working day. After all, in the US where productivity per man-hour is said to be about twice our own, people do not appear to be enjoying more leisure.[4] How could we possibly hope to compete in world markets? What choice have we but to return to the treadmill?

This is a sad state for any nation to be in, and in an affluent society surpassingly strange: to have come this far into the twentieth century with economists interpreting the alleged increase in our real income as 'enrichment' or, more sagaciously, as 'an extension of the area of choice', and then to be told almost daily that we have no choice; that if we are to pay our way in the world we must work harder than ever. This is enough surely to tax the credulity of any being whose judgement has not yet been swept away by torrents of economic exhortation.

But of course we have a choice, a wide range of choice! The main purpose of this essay is to uncover the kinds of choices that face us, or any modern community, and to make it apparent that the so-called policy of economic growth as popularly understood is hardly more than a policy of drifting quickly – of snatching at any technological innovation that proves marketable with scant respect for the social consequences.

In the formulation of the ends of economic policy the word *need* is not to be invoked. Markets do not *need* to expand – although, of course, businessmen dearly like to see them expand (whether through increasing *per capita* income, increasing domestic population or increased immigration). It is quite possible to arrange things so as to produce a good deal fewer gadgets and instead to enjoy more leisure. And, although blasphemous to

4. In this connection see T. Scitovsky 'What Price Economic Progress', *Yale Review*, 1959 (reprinted in *Papers on Welfare and Growth*, Allen & Unwin, London, 1964).

utter, it is also possible to train fewer scientists and engineers without our perishing from the face of the earth. Nor do we *need* to capture world markets in the hope of being able to lower costs; or to lower costs in the hope of capturing world markets. We can, while acting as rational beings, deliberately choose to reduce our foreign trade and in some lines, therefore, to produce smaller quantities at a somewhat higher cost. We can even decide to reduce the strains of competition and opt for an easier life. All these choices and many others can be translated into perfectly practicable alternatives whenever public opinion is ready to consider them. And I have no objection to our bright young men dubbing all suggested alternatives to the sweat-and-strain doctrine as 'irresponsible' provided they agree to use the word *want* instead of *need*. This simple switch of words will serve to remind us that policies radically different from those we habitually pursue are actually open to us all the time – though some people may well feel uncertain of, or disapprove of, some of their consequences.

III

There follows a digression on the balance of payments which the reader may omit on a first reading. It was felt necessary to make a brief incursion into this territory because of the disproportionate attention paid to foreign trade in our newspapers, and because of such widespread fallacies as the belief that we have to work harder if we are to 'pay our way' in the world, or the belief that unless we grow faster we shall run further into international debt or become 'insolvent'. Such fallacies render the public more vulnerable to the thesis of the hard-boiled school, that we have no choice but to thrust ahead vigorously, and render them more tolerant, therefore, of those growing disamenities inflicted on society by the tacit acceptance of purely commercial criteria.

The Balance of Payments (i)

THE substitution of government exhortation for economic policy is a feature of our national life particular to the postwar period, and though fairly popular in other countries whenever economic difficulties are encountered it has had so great a fashion in Britain that one discerns a tradition in the making. Crying wolf at the drop of an index, discovering ourselves edgily perched at the precipice every other year, lectured round the clock about our shortcomings as 'economic men' (while in between times being taken to task for our crass materialism), continually being warned that we cannot go on much longer 'living beyond our means'[1] – and yet in some mysterious manner able apparently to put off the dread day of reckoning indefinitely – it is not surprising that our responsiveness, alike to pep-talks and to crisis-talks, has waned over the years. We seem to have learned to live comfortably in an atmosphere of vague but persistent economic foreboding.

This is as well as may be. What is amiss is the common belief that the concern with growth, with inflation, and with the balance of payments is the very stuff of modern economics; furthermore, that the figures for annual productivity, interest rates, exchange reserves, are the indicators *par excellence* of our material comfort,

1. Our current excess of imports, between £250 million and £400 million per annum, represents no more than between 1 per cent and $1\frac{1}{2}$ per cent of our total national income, and well below the average per annum real increase of national income. The notion, therefore, that only hard work and austere living will enable us 'to pay our way' in the world is nonsense. It may be difficult to coax foreigners to buy that little extra of our goods that would bring us into balance, but if they were willing to buy the extra we need endure no hardship in supplying them. If not, again without hardship, we could directly reduce our excess imports, or, as we shall see, invest abroad less than we have been doing.

the very substance if not the sum total of our national achievement. It is just this sort of belief that makes economics so exasperating a subject to the layman and acts over time to cramp the vision of men in authority. It is this sort of belief that imbues otherwise intelligent people with a compelling sense of urgency, so that once in office they cannot forbear to warn, to cajole and to bribe us and to threaten us about increasing this, that and the other. It is this sort of belief that prevents ministers and officials from thinking anew and critically about our existing economic institutions. For despite pop journalistic phrases about 'new thinking', 'cool looks', 'radical reorganizations', 'agonizing reappraisals', and the like, there is hardly an unorthodox idea about economics to be found lurking in the 'establishment', or for that matter in the 'anti-establishment'. Especially is this true about our notions of foreign trade.

To touch, by way of example, on a minor issue first – the connexion between economic growth and the balance of payments. If we are exhorted to export more, we are no less exhorted to grow faster. More exports and more productivity are both 'good things' and, what is more, the success of either, it is believed, is promoted by the success of the other. If we grow faster we shall, we are told, improve our export position. And if we export more, this will surely enable us to grow more swiftly. We seem, therefore, to have two good reasons for keeping our attention riveted on either.

These supposed connexions do not, however, stand up to cursory examination. Suppose we are so charmed with the speech of Mr Shovehard, the Minister for Exports, that we all decide to abandon our union, or private, demarcation rules and instead to work overtime to make our goods more attractive in price and quality to the foreigners, and suppose also that we succeed thereby in reversing the present trade balance into one of a large export surplus. However, in making such goods attractive to foreigners we have also made them more plentiful and attractive to ourselves, a factor which must be chalked up to the growth account. But this increase in our exports has not caused the increase in growth; rather it appears as an incidental effect of economic growth as evinced by reduced prices and improved quality. We seem to have shown the reverse causal relationship: that growth leads to exports. This, however, is an incomplete account and we shall return to it in a moment. In the meantime, in order effectively to isolate the exports-helps-growth thesis, suppose instead that by some happy accident unforeseen by economists exports grow rapidly so that soon we are able to show a large export surplus year after year. Does this of itself promote economic growth? One reason why it may do the reverse is that while our export surplus is maintained it will be financed by an equal reduction of our available gross domestic saving and, therefore, a reduction to that extent of investment in domestic industry. Conversely, so long as an import surplus is maintained it enables us to release domestic resources in order to add to the new investment already made available by domestic saving. Economic analysis can go further than this, of course, but enough has been said to suggest that a statement that economic growth is itself helped along by an expansion of exports is not a self-evident piece of reasoning.

As for the reverse relation: that of economic growth stimulating exports, although the assertion has a superficial plausibility – as, for instance, in the first half of the above paragraph – this relation, too, tends to wilt under scrutiny. The effects on our balance of payments of an increase in the rate of economic growth may be considered under two main headings, (1) the aggregative and (2) the technological. Under (1) we include two general propositions: (a) inasmuch as this country spends a given fraction of its income on imports, a faster growth of its real income from any cause – increasing population, increasing *per capita* income with, or without, technological advance – results in a faster growth of its imports from the rest of the world; (b) in so far as the level of our prices rises compared with the price-levels of other countries this fraction of our income spent on imports itself tends to rise (and the fraction the world spends on our exports to fall), thus aggravating further an adverse balance of payments. And our price-level may well rise, both absolutely and relative to world prices, if the increase in our rate of growth is accompanied by attempts to push further into our 'full-employment zone'.

Under (2) we take account of the effects of improved technology on the prices of our import substitutes and on the prices of our exports. (*a*) If the spurt in productivity chiefly takes the form of innovations in the domestic production of new or cheaper substitutes for our imports, the volume and the value of our imports are thereby reduced. (*b*) On the other hand, if our productivity advances are concentrated in our export industries, then although the *volume* of our exports will tend to increase, their *value* will increase only if, despite our lower prices, foreigners spend more of their currency on them. Should they spend less on them (increasing their purchases by a proportion that is smaller than the fall in our prices) the value of our exports will fall.

As it happens, the quantitative information necessary to strike a balance of tendency for the UK is, as yet, unavailable. Until it becomes available there can be no acceptable presumption that, in general, a faster rate of economic growth in the UK would improve the balance of payments position. In the meantime, however, it is my guess that it would be likely to worsen the balance of payments.

Let us then turn to a more fundamental problem, the importance to our economy of a large volume of trade. The public, long conditioned by their newspapers, are in no doubt that we must export to 'survive'. If we have managed to survive for so long without exporting enough to 'pay our way' in the world, it is presumably because the world has been lenient with us so far. The transition from export-mindedness to mercantilism is, however, short and easy. It is not uncommon for large export orders, gained or lost, to make front-page news. Apparently goods exported emit an odour of sanctity denied to common or garden goods that remain to be consumed inside the country. The impression persists that by exporting we pile up reserves of economic strength along with foreign currencies, and that by importing we dissipate them. An announcement from the Board of Trade that the country's exports are breaking all records has a regenerative effect on our spirits: we begin to feel proud, confident and very respectable. One dares not imagine the general acclaim and exhilaration that would follow the discovery, at the end of the year, that we had in fact exported the whole of our national output.

Now businessmen need seldom trouble to push their ideas to their logical conclusions. They know that more of some things is good and more of other things is bad. Without a shadow of doubt, exports are one of the good things: it follows that we cannot really have enough of them. The trained economist, how-ever, has at the fore of his mind the notion of an 'optimum' quantity or flow of things. The 'optimum' volume of trade would be the 'just right' volume (in a sense to be indicated later[2]) more than which, or less, is to be avoided. Though this concept is straightforward enough, as we shall see, owing to a highly volatile economic environment this optimum volume of foreign trade is practically impossible to measure with a pretence of anything approaching exactness. For all that, the notion of an optimum volume of trade as a goal of attainment could with advantage replace the current mercantilist view rampant among businessmen, journalists and politicians. It would increase their receptiveness to the possibility, the likelihood even, that the volume of our foreign trade is too large; that we should be more comfortable with a smaller volume of trade.

It is not necessary in this essay, however, to burden the reader with the theory of optimal tariffs which demonstrates that, start-ing from a free trade equilibrium, there exists a set of tariffs that (in the absence of retaliation) would enable the community to exploit the maximum advantage from its foreign trade and, in any case, attain a higher level of potential welfare than would exist in a completely free trade situation. Nevertheless, by translating into welfare terms the two related effects of a tariff – a reduction in the domestic demand for imports and the consequent improve-ment in the terms of trade – such theorems do serve to combat parochial doctrine about the advantages of increasing foreign trade.

In the existing circumstances, however, it is more relevant to

2. In the digression on marginal cost pricing.

consider ways of reducing the volume of imports,[3] and of stabilizing its composition, with the object of diminishing the magnitude and recurrence of balance-of-payment crises in a world of fixed exchange rates. A discussion of this possibility has the incidental merit of exposing in another crucial context the falseness of the no-choice myth. There are no 'musts' in international trade, as in fact there are none in the field of economic policy. 'Export or perish' slogans are a misleading form of rhetoric. Economics is concerned, *inter alia*, with investigating the implications of *alternative* choices that are open to us. And if presumably honest men talk to us as if there is in fact no choice, they do so either in ignorance of the opportunities that are open to us or else from the conviction – which occasionally, at least, ought to be made explicit – that we should concur with them in rejecting all the alternatives did we but know them.

Turning, therefore, to the volume of foreign trade, we might begin by agreeing that, given the already outsize population of these islands, there would be genuine hardship for a long time if we could not import some minimum assortment of goods from abroad. Whatever our conception of this minimum assortment, once we extend the import ration from this bare minimum we move out of the range of discomfort and enter a range of diminishing frustration. The ration now includes goods that are generally admitted to be highly desirable. We move on from there to include the range of fashion and luxury goods: French cheeses, Italian shoes, German cars, Belgian chocolate, American cigarettes, Japanese toys, Dutch tomatoes, and so on; things not to be spurned, and important for a variety of reasons to some people, but which could be called 'essential' only by a misleading use of language. Yet if a sizeable proportion of our import bill does consist of goods such as these that cannot reasonably be classified as 'essential', and indeed may more usefully be classified as 'expendable', it is surely perverse that responsible ministers should continue to exhort us as though such imports were a

3. It is generally recognized that the elimination of a deficit by import controls is less 'burdensome' than its elimination by exports promotion. See Appendix B.

matter of life and death to our economy. Of course, they do not say this in so many words; rather they talk about the country's need to *export*, and labour us with patriotic duty to strain to the utmost to sell abroad. But the additional exports we must strain ourselves to sell can be properly regarded as 'essential' to our 'solvency' only in so far as our imports of close substitutes and luxuries and quasi-luxuries are themselves essential.[4]

Ordinary honesty should make it clear to the public that we have, for one reason or another, adopted the policy of allowing the import of 'expendable' goods, and in consequence we are now seemingly up against the wall trying, at the given rate of exchange, to pay for them with exports. For all I know such a policy if understood by the public might be universally approved – another challenge, perhaps! But since these simple implications of our current foreign trade policy are never put to the public in this candid fashion, we have no means of knowing what the response of the public would be.[5]

One of the things that we import to the tune of some £300 million a year (taking an average over the last six years) that cannot by any stretch of imagination be called essential is foreign securities[6] – in other words, lending abroad or the export of capital.[7] Moreover, this is one kind of import which, if curtailed, is not in the least likely to cause reprisals.

4. In general, it is misleading to assert that we *need* to export, say, an additional £200 million in order to meet the excess of our imports unless it is agreed that *everything* we imports is *needed* in that same sense.

5. While it is true that we have certain international commitments and that unilateral action of some sort and on some scale would invite retaliation, there is no reason to speak and act as though we were tied hand and foot by the rest of the world, and unable to move a joint save by international consensus. It is possible that the continuance of our traditional policies carries more depressing consequences than those that would follow our opting out of international agreements (if necessary). However, as we shall see, there are other, more radical choices yet available to us.

6. It is true that the import of securities may lead to export orders. But the fraction of exports thereby generated qualifies the magnitude only, not the essential argument.

7. Any interest or dividends collected in this country over the future do feature as part of our invisible exports. They must therefore be taken into

In addition, there are longer term allocative implications that suggest a reduction of our capital exports, at least if we are concerned with the economic position of the domestic economy.[8] It may well be that the British investor's immediate expectations are realized and he obtains a higher return from his capital abroad than he does by investing it in the home economy. However, as additional capital is exported its yield abroad diminishes. In general this causes the yield on all the intra-marginal units of capital, already exported, to diminish also. Thus, the net return to a marginal unit of capital is less than what is received by the investor of that marginal unit by an amount equal to the fall in the return on all previously exported units of capital. Indeed, the net return to the domestic economy of the additional unit of capital exported might well be negative.[9]

There are two other reasons why investment abroad tends to be too high relative to domestic investment. The first arises from the process of innovation. In so far as technologically more advanced capital equipment is introduced in the production of specific goods the prices of such goods (relative to other goods and relative to wages) tend to fall. As a result, the return on any previous investment of now-obsolescent capital also tends to fall. The investor is aware of this risk of obsolescence but is indifferent to incurring the risk at home or abroad. But the domestic economy ought not to be indifferent. Within the domestic economy such

account in any long-term policy. But we are concerned here with the immediate and short-term balance of payments problem.

8. If, on the other hand, we are concerned quite selflessly with the welfare of the world at large, we should seek to increase international factor mobility – encouraging the export of our capital especially to underdeveloped countries and importing their labour – until some international equilibrium is reached.

9. For the world economy as a whole this reduction in the returns of all intra-marginal units represents a transfer from the owners of capital to the rest of the population. But from the standpoint of the capital-exporting country, the fall in the return on the intra-marginal units of capital already exported is to be regarded as an external diseconomy. For the additional investor unwittingly inflicts a loss on all the existing holders of foreign capital. Such a loss would be taken into account only if the export of capital were in the hands of a monopoly.

losses suffered by the domestic investor represent a gain for the domestic population. If, on the other hand, the investment is placed abroad, any such subsequent loss represents a transfer from the domestic capitalist to the foreign population.

The third reason for the tendency to over-invest abroad arises from institutional factors. The rational investor compares the returns to his investment at home and abroad net of all taxes. Now the return to the British economy of an increment of investment abroad is in fact no more than the return received by the British investor after paying taxes to the foreign government. The return to the British economy of investment at home, on the other hand, exceeds the net return received by the British investor by the amount of the tax he pays to the British Government.

The case for the control of foreign investment is even stronger than these long-term considerations suggest, when such investment is seen against the backcloth of continual balance-of-payments difficulties. For this search by investors for larger profits abroad is what ultimately contributes to bringing about the credit restrictions at home, to say nothing of our government having to borrow abroad, on short term, at very high rates.[10]

Another practical way of reducing our imports is to grow more of our foodstuffs at home. Increased self-sufficiency in foodstuffs (after allowance for the import-content of increased home production) may save us well over £100 million of imports and, possibly, without much increase in costs. Farming is one of Britain's more efficient industries, and if there were some initial rise in costs it would probably be absorbed within a few years. In the short run, moreover, import restrictions might well lower the foreign price of our remaining food imports since some time must elapse before foreign supplies find other suitable outlets.

Finally, as one looks down the list of items imported into, and exported from, the UK, one is invariably struck by the close re-

10. It does not follow from these remarks that no foreign investment should be permitted; merely that the bulk of our foreign lending should not be determined by the profit expectations of investors, but rather by more comprehensive welfare criteria and/or by considerations bearing on the country's long-term economic policy.

semblance between them. Textiles, clothing, footwear, hardware, automobiles, ships, trucks, aircraft, paints, machinery of all kinds, cameras, toys, and vast quantities of chemicals are both imported and exported. One could reasonably surmise that a large proportion of these things, in particular the finished goods, are very close substitutes, and that although their further restriction might cause some occasional resentment – and would certainly incur the charge of retrograde among the doctrinaire – it would not be likely to inflict hardship.[11] At any rate, increased restrictions on these luxuries, quasi-luxuries, and close substitutes would, in the immediate short run at least, reduce the apparent need to whip ourselves into 'viability'. However, this proposal to examine ways and means of reducing our present import bill, it should be stressed, is not for the purpose of gaining any ephemeral trade advantage. True, the immediate effect of implementing the proposed measures might be regarded as an attempt to cut our foreign purchases to what we could comfortably afford, and as such one need not alarm oneself with exaggerated expectations of retaliation. But the larger objective is to reduce permanently the volume of our foreign trade and, perhaps, to induce other Western European countries to do the same. By eliminating much – just how much can be left to discussion – of the trade in luxuries, close substitutes and such goods as one might reasonably classify as expendable, one could hope for greater stability in the pattern and volume of trade over the future. One might hope therefore to check the present trend towards an increasingly fluctuating pattern of foreign trade, especially as by far the greater part of world trade takes place between the affluent countries of the West, and as a proportion of world trade is increasing. On the supply side, more rapidly advancing technology entails a swifter shifting to and fro of short-lived technological advantage in closely competitive products – and, with larger productive units, the competition is likely to be pretty ruthless. On the demand side, as the margin for non-essentials grows over the future, one may surely anticipate more impulse- and fashion-buying, features that

11. I would say that not less than £800 million of our yearly imports come into this category.

can only aggravate the increasing vicissitudes of international trade. Of course, there will always be those who view the fierce competitive struggle with exhilaration. To others, who see in life more serious objectives than a perpetual jockeying for position, the opportunity of permanently reducing the least stable, or most expendable, components of our imports by some sacrifice of variety and perhaps cheapness, in order to remain free from perpetual anxiety, may have a stronger appeal.[12]

12. It will always be argued by the inveterate free trader that the competition of such foreign goods, whether Italian Fiats, or French frocks, helps to keep down domestic prices. However, the size of the British home market alone is, for practically all of those sorts of imports, large enough to exploit fully the economies of scale. Where the efficient plant size is small enough it is up to the Government to make much more use of the Monopolies Commission and the Restrictive Practices Court in promoting competition. Where not, product standardization, either voluntary or government-inspired, may enable us to reduce costs without much sacrifice – or, indeed, with some welcome sacrifice – of variety.

The Balance of Payments (ii)

WHEN one bears in mind the disproportionate influence exerted by foreign trade in our domestic affairs, and the absorption of time and financial talent in the endless task of 'maintaining the strength of the pound', one is tempted to suggest measures that are more radical yet than a deliberate reduction in our volume of trade. It is surely worth paying a high price in order to end once and for all time this perverse phenomenon of the foreign-trade tail wagging the domestic economy. Indeed, it would be an act of emancipation, if not of mercy, to free successive governments from unceasing preoccupation with the balance of payments and thus to provide them with the time and breathing space necessary to look around and discover what is happening to the country.

Two alternative policies to the present system which could contribute substantially to this desideratum are (a) state-trading, and (b) a freely flexible pound, proposals that can be expected with confidence to meet with a dusty reception from the press if only for the reason that either treads heavily on material, intellectual and ideological interests. None the less, if we are to take seriously the popular slogan about 'facing up to the twentieth century' both are worthy of more public attention than they receive.

I use the term state-trading reluctantly, aware of the antagonism it arouses in the breasts of those who equate personal freedom with the operation of free markets and perceive sinister possibilities in any extension of state enterprise. Yet no more is intended here than the establishment of a state-trading agency with powers to enter into long-term contracts with other countries (on a bilateral or multilateral basis) in order to ensure the means of paying for adequate supplies, in some sense, of foodstuffs, raw materials and other 'priority' goods. Such an agency would adopt some method for appointing domestic firms to meet its long-term export contracts and some method (possibly auctioning) of disposing of its imports to domestic wholesalers. One may reasonably assume, in addition, that there would still be frequent opportunities for supplementing the variety of imports by further bargains between countries.

This is not the place to develop a detailed description of the operation of such an agency, nor to defend it against the familiar objections – the rigidity and ponderousness of such public agencies in contrast to the alleged flexibility and variety of the existing private enterprise system. Indeed, one would be pleasantly surprised if such a state body managed entirely to escape such defects. But such ponderousness, if it were irreducible, would be acknowledged as part of the price we should be willing to pay in order to unchain our domestic economic policy from the inescapable vagaries of unhindered privately conducted trade at fixed exchange rates.

It is to be understood that such an agency should for the most part confine its long-term contracts to ensuring 'essential' imports, with the option of shopping around for bargains in the less essential goods. The import of additional 'luxury' goods might also be allowed by selling in a free market any excess of foreign earnings. This possibility brings us to the other proposal: the attempt to establish a freely fluctuating pound – the price of the pound, in terms of foreign currencies, moving continually so as to equate the demand for sterling (in exchange for foreign currencies) with its current supply, irrespective of the domestic policy the Government chooses to pursue.

Under such an institution the Government *need* no longer hold reserves of gold of foreign currencies,[1] for it has no obligation to

1. Though the Government does not need to hold any reserves, there is much to be said for its continuing, for several years, to use exchange reserves to iron out random, seasonal, and other irrelevant exchange fluctuations that might occur during a transitional period during which the foreign exchange market was growing in the expertise and resources necessary to free the Government completely from further concern with the exchange rate.

maintain the price of sterling on world markets. And no consideration of an external balance can prevent it, at all times, from pursuing the monetary and fiscal policy that seems appropriate to the domestic situation.[2] In principle, the mechanism is simple: if at the existing exchange rate our demand for foreign currency persistently exceeds foreigners' demand for our currency, the value of the pound would tend to fall, and would continue to fall until – our goods having become cheaper in terms of foreigners' currencies (and foreign goods having become dearer in terms of sterling) – equilibrium is restored.[3]

Although our experience of flexible exchange rates is very limited there is nothing in the brief British experience – between 1919 and 1924 and again from 1931, when we were forced off gold by panic flights of capital, until the Tripartite Pact of 1936 – or in the recent Canadian experience, between 1950 and 1962 (during which period, although the Canadian dollar was nominally free to float, the Government intervened to 'smooth out'

2. The existence of some £4 billion sterling balances held by foreigners, the greater part by governments, clearly poses a problem. But a problem would have to be very many times more difficult than this for it to weigh as a serious objection against so far-reaching an experiment. Obviously, some arrangement involving, say, an exchange guarantee would have to be reached with the chief countries holding sterling balances in order to avoid, during the first few years of the experiment, any prolonged downward pressure on the pound arising from the efforts of large holders of sterling to convert their holdings into other currencies.

3. The greater part of our demand for foreign currencies arises, of course, from our demand for foreign goods and services. The less responsive is our demand for imports and the less responsive is the foreign demand for our exports, with respect to movements in the rate of exchange, the larger the required change in the price of sterling for any autonomous shift in demand. There has always been much controversy over the actual degree of responsiveness of imports and exports to changes in the exchange rates. Attempts to estimate the elasticity of foreign demand for the goods of any particular country have not brought agreement any closer. It must be admitted, however, that the less responsive these demands are the more difficult the scheme will be to work. If there were good reasons to believe that very large movements of the exchange rate had little effect on the respective demands for currency, one would tend to favour state-trading in 'essentials', leaving the less essentials and 'luxuries' to free exchanges, since for these latter goods price-responsiveness is generally believed to be high.

erratic movements), which gives ground for the oft voiced suspicion that a freely floating pound would be unstable; that is, the exchange rate would fluctuate so wildly as to seriously damage the international exchange of goods. Nor does this limited experience provide any evidence for the view that a flexible exchange rate, of itself, is likely to impart an inflationary momentum to the economy.

To those wedded to the *status quo* every conceivable misadventure associated with a radical change of policy is depicted as though it were a veritable certainty, while the encumbrances daily inflicted upon us by the existing policy are barely mentioned. The hypothetical dangers[4] are thus highly overrated compared with the quite certain and palpable disadvantages of maintaining a fixed exchange rate in a world which can look increasingly to more rapid shiftings of the pattern of international trade. Moreover, neither of the contingencies feared, allowing they took place, is so dangerous as to prohibit some experiment along these lines. No matter what the uncertainty surrounding the future movements of the pound, it is hardly likely that the volume of trade would be much reduced since it will always be open to traders to hedge against risks by selling or buying foreign exchange in organized forward exchange markets.[5]

4. Two other popular objections to flexible exchange rates may be worth mentioning:

(1) Since forward markets are limited to short-term transactions, there would be no institutional mechanisms to cover exchange risks incurred by long-term foreign investment which might, therefore, start to fall off. However, an addition of, say, one per cent per annum extra return on a fifteen to twenty-five year investment would be more than enough to compensate for the risk of very large changes in the rate of exchange.

(2) Flexible exchange rates, it is alleged, may cause fluctuations in the foreign demand for the products of our export industries so reducing their efficient growth. However, this contingency must be compared with their fate under a rigid pound backed by relatively low exchange reserves. The resulting 'stop-go' policies with which we are familiar are yet more damaging since they affect not merely the export industries but practically all industries in the economy.

5. Not, of course, that it would matter much if the volume of trade were

As for the instability of a freely moving exchange rate, if we mean by that term wide fluctuations within short periods, the likelihood is greater: (1) the greater the proportion of the total transactions in the currency is for speculative purposes as distinct from trading purposes,[6] (2) the more volatile and erratic are the expectations of speculators,[7] and (3) the less responsive is the direction of trade to changes in the value of the currency. Much therefore depends upon the 'real' forces – the response of our imports and exports to a change in the international value of the pound – and the organization of the foreign exchange market. Stability increases according to the size of the market for foreign exchange, the accuracy of the information at its disposal, and the ability of professional speculators to forecast correctly. Although, as indicated, the historical experience on which any sober judgement of the likely course of events is lacking, two considerations seem to augur well for the experiment. First, existing commodity markets have served the community well: it is generally believed that in their absence commodity prices would fluctuate more steeply than they do. Of course prices fluctuate sharply enough even on such well organized markets, but this is unavoidable since the supply of the crop is usually fixed by the harvest for some time, and also because the ultimate demand for it is usually highly inelastic. These conditions are not present in international trade and one may reasonably expect the proportional fluctuations will be less. Secondly, fears of wild fluctuations, as also fears of continued decline in the international value of the

---

somewhat reduced. The essentials in trade would easily weather any residual uncertainty, which uncertainty would have more of a damping effect on the import of 'expendables – goods having a relatively high elasticity of import demand and a relatively low 'welfare content'.

6. This is a functional distinction, since to some extent the exporter, or importer, is, or may become, a speculator.

7. In general, all price expectations may be regarded as destabilizing within limits (a rise in price, for instance, leading to expectations of a further rise in price) and stabilizing outside these limits (a rise in price leading to expectations that the price will return to a lower level). The wider these limits the more destabilizing are expectations.

pound,[8] should be brought into relation with the fact that at least there is no need for these things. We were, after all, able to maintain a quite rigid exchange rate for some seventeen years without apparent calamity. Stresses and strains there were, and some trying moments also. But the stark fact that we were able to continue without any change at all in the exchange rate for seventeen years strongly suggests that large and frequent changes are not necessary. Much, however, depends upon the way we

8. Though much is made of the possibility of a 'ratchet effect' – a wage cost inflation taking place whenever the value of the pound fell and import prices rose, with no symmetrical reduction of wages when the pound rose and import prices fell – it is difficult to believe that the day-to-day fluctuations of the exchange would have that much impact on the cost-of-living index, which would rise noticeably only if there were a persistent trend against the pound. Even so we must remember that a 4–5 per cent rise in the cost of living maintained over a year or so and caused only by imports would require an average rise in their prices of over 20 per cent.

There are two main reasons why import prices could rise appreciably. For structural reasons: e.g. a rise in the UK demand for certain types of foreign goods (because of a change in taste), or a long-term reduction in foreign supplies, will lower the value of the freely fluctuating pound. The consequent rise in import prices under these circumstances would, however, also take place under fixed exchange rates. The other reason for rising import prices is the general substitution of foreign goods for British goods as a consequence of an already existing inflation in the UK. Whereas with a fixed exchange rate rising domestic prices cause a switch of demand from domestic goods for foreign goods thereby generating an import surplus, which enables us to pass on to other countries some of our inflationary pressure, flexible exchange rates act instead to contain the domestic inflation by causing the prices of foreign goods to rise along with those of our domestic goods. However, if we cannot 'export' some of our inflation, neither can we 'import' any – the insulation works both ways, and to that extent puts the burden of domestic policy where it should rightly be, entirely on the domestic economy.

Obviously, then, a policy of flexible exchange rates does not of itself promote price-stability. If industries are willing and, as a result of the Government's ineffectual monetary policy, able, to make continued concessions to the unions in the belief that in times of creeping inflation higher prices are easily passed on to the public, a change to flexible exchange rates will not suffice to alter this entrepreneurial behaviour. However, just because we can no longer run into debt and head for a balance of payments crisis, the consequences of ineffectual monetary policy are immediate and wholly visible.

make the transition to free exchanges. Thus, granted that setting up a free market in foreign currencies would be a much larger undertaking than setting up an organized commodity market, one should be able to count on the Government's initial support of the experiment, first by launching the venture when the pound was fairly strong and, secondly, by using its existing reserves to iron out the wilder speculative movements until such time as the market grew in skill and resources and was able to stand comfortably on its own feet.

The fears of strong speculative pressure are in fact a legacy not of a period of flexible exchanges but of a period of pegged exchange rates which, by providing any amateur with plenty of time to observe events, consult the obvious figures, and ponder the degree of unanimity of the experts, veritably invites the non-specialized public to take up a safe option. If a balance-of-payments deficit continues to use up exchange reserves for several consecutive years to the manifest concern of the Government, one stands to lose very little by selling sterling, spot or forward, if the pound is not depreciated, and to gain a great deal if, after all, it is depreciated. These one-way options, a boon to ordinary businessmen and a curse to governments trying to maintain pegged rates, cannot without the strictest capital controls be dissociated from a system of fixed exchange rates. The relevant generalization, in fact, is: the higher the degree of exchange flexibility the smaller the opportunity for the parasitic speculation that is such a pronounced feature of the system of fixed exchanges.

At this stage, one should recognize the more cautious proposals that are put forward from time to time to ease us away from the rigidly fixed exchange rate; for instance, that the degree of flexibility of the pound should be limited to a rise or fall of 2 per cent per annum, in effect limiting the movement of the pound to a maximum of 4 per cent within a year, a maximum speculative gain that could, if necessary, be offset by a differential in the interest rates between this country and others. Such proposals move in the right direction[9] and would be an improvement over

9. This 'wider band' proposal and/or a 'sliding parity' (allowing a discretion to any country, under revised IMF rules, to change the rate of exchange

the present system in giving some increased flexibility to domestic policy. But only as we move on to the bolder scheme of complete flexibility do we confer independence on our domestic economic policy.[10]

Although much has been written on this question of exchange rate flexibility the conclusions reached have always been much influenced by basic ideologies and one's estimates of political 'realities'–which estimates sometimes go with a strong preference for inertia as against initiative and experiment. An unbroken period of fixed exchange rates with all the day-to-day, week-to-week and year-to-year preoccupation with these thorny, albeit familiar, problems about stockpiling, seasonal variations, 'leads and lags', the movements of gold and the exchange reserves, foreign confidence and central-bank cooperation, to say nothing of a succession of international conferences with endless proposals for increasing international liquidity and expanding international trade, all this has created stubborn material and intellectual interests. The cumulated weight of years of habitual response lies heavy on our spirit, and though our political leaders follow the fashion and croak 'challenge' from time to time there has been no response in terms of political ingenuity. For the recurring ailment nothing but more of the same old medicine: sweat, toil and exhortations to export.

---

by, say, one sixth of one per cent each month if a deficit, or a surplus, continues to appear) among other proposals have been briefly discussed by Professor J. E. Meade in two articles (*The Three Banks Review*, September 1964 and June 1966). The one serious objection to the wider band proposal is that, in order to avoid speculative pressure against the currency of the deficit country, interest rate differentials as between the deficit and surplus countries must be such as to offset potential speculative gains. Since the deficit country has to raise its short-term interest rates in these circumstances it is denied the free use of the one weapon that it should be making more use of in pursuit of a domestic policy of full employment with price stability.

10. While it is true that changes in the direction of international trade may affect the domestic price level, and also that changes in domestic policy may affect the pattern of international trade, even with a system of flexible exchange rates, under such a system the Government *need* concentrate only on domestic policy.

The aim of this brief discussion has been limited to persuading readers of the habitual magnification of the balance-of-payments problem and the error residing in the conventional belief that we have no choice at all but to export or go under in a world in which some sort of critical 'race' is on, one from which we cannot hope to escape. In the following pages we make no further reference to international trade, not because there are no incidental balance-of-payments effects flowing from one sort of domestic policy as against some other, but because the crux of the balance-of-payments problem, as seen here, is the psychological one of being unable to break free from long-established habits of thought. Until we are ready to dare to think unorthodox thoughts we must dismiss as illusory any hope of being able, permanently, to emancipate domestic policy from the vicissitude of international trade and capital movements.

We turn now to consider the very real choices that are open to us here and now, regarding ourselves, realistically, as a wealthy and resourceful country.

3

The Choices Open to Us

IN the light of the preceding remarks let us reconsider the question of emphasis among the three components of long-term economic policy:

(1) *Economic Growth.* Though no economist who has studied the relation between economics and social welfare would endorse a policy of economic growth without an embarrassing amount of qualification, the profession as a whole behaves as if, on balance, it was a good thing. This attitude may spring from an impatience with quasi-philosophical inquiries that unavoidably call into question the usefulness of much of the highly skilled economic research currently undertaken. But there is room also for rationalization. One of the more obvious pretexts for pressing on regardless is the existence of poverty in the greater part of the world: in Asia, in Africa, and in large parts of South America. There are pockets of degrading poverty even within the wealthy countries though, as indicated earlier, their continuation may be attributed ultimately to political prejudices, not to economic necessity.[1]

Now if the rich countries, in response to a moral challenge, sought to convert themselves into an arsenal to provision the hungry areas of Asia and Africa, a case could be made for retaining economic growth as the chief goal of economic policy for some considerable time. But though magniloquence on the foreign aid theme marks all fitting occasions, the scale of such aid to poor countries in the postwar period is more suggestive, to use

1. If within these wealthy countries the public conscience is unperturbed by the existence of a small minority of very poor people, many of whom are too old or too sick to take care of themselves, we might as well admit it. It is hypocrisy to pretend that the only way to help them is to create more wealth by growing faster when, in fact, the share of the underprivileged minority in the annual increment of output is negligible.

62

Professor Bauer's words, of 'conscience money' than of moral commitment. When we bear in mind that the total aid given to poor countries by the largest donor, the United States, a country that is struggling continuously with problems of near-surfeit, does not amount to as much as one per cent of its Gross National Product, one has no choice but to reject this justification out of hand.[2]

The belief that only a faster economic growth will enable any country to 'pay its way in the world', or that faster growth generates more exports, hardly stands up to analysis. In any case they were shown to be erroneous in the Digression on the Balance of Payments. Neither does the view that our ability to survive a military attack depends on our rate of economic growth carry conviction. If it were felt that the country's chance of repelling an enemy attack in the foreseeable future would be distinctly improved by augmenting our weapons supply and by improving our war technology, we could achieve these things more directly by shifting a large proportion of our national resources into the production of weapons and into more intensive scientific research for defence. It is, of course, possible to believe that a change in the growth rate from between 2 and $2\frac{1}{2}$ per cent to between 3 and $3\frac{1}{2}$ per cent would have the incidental effect of enabling us better to withstand enemy attacks. But no one surely would be rash enough to argue that the goal of faster growth is justified solely, or even largely, by defence considerations.

We fall back then on the more popular and explicit belief that a *per capita* rise in real income is a good thing in itself; that in

2. The limited ability of these poor countries to absorb aid and the balance-of-payments problem are sometimes invoked to explain the glaringly inadequate contribution of the West. Neither factor carries conviction. There may indeed be difficulties of persuading indigenous populations to use Western techniques and of training them to operate modern machinery. But there should be no difficulty in supplying the direct needs of people – foodstuffs, clothing, medical supplies, pesticides, contraceptives and farm implements – in order to alleviate distress. As for the balance-of-payments problem, if the US guaranteed to provide, say, 10 per cent of its annual income to India, that country would be glad to accept it as a tied gift – that is, subject to the condition that the dollars received be spent entirely in the USA.

expanding the range of opportunities for ordinary people it increases their welfare. It will not, however, be difficult to uncover serious weaknesses in this common presumption, enough at any rate to warrant a conclusion that economic growth *per se* is a component of policy on which the least emphasis should be placed if we are interested primarily in social welfare.

Indices of economic growth may measure, in a rough sort of way, the increase in a country's gross productive power. But no provision is made in such indices for the 'negative goods' that are also being increased; that is, for the increasing burden of disamenities in the country. Nor can they reveal certain imponderable but none the less crucial consequences associated with the indiscriminate pursuit of technological progress, about which something will be said in the last part of this book. Indeed, the adoption of economic growth as a primary aim of policy, whether it is urged upon us as a moral duty to the rest of the world or as a duty to posterity, or as a condition of survival, seems on reflection as likely to add, at least, as much 'ill-fare' as welfare to society. Certainly there can be no purely economic justification for a policy of growth *per se*. The simple view that it 'enrichens' society, or that it expands the range of choice open to mankind, stands up neither to argument nor to the facts of common experience – unless, of course, words such as 'enrichen' or 'expanding choices' are made to carry the same meaning as an increase of productive potential which is, roughly, what the index of productivity seeks to measure. If, however, we are concerned with social welfare in the ordinary sense, the only legitimate procedure is to consider consequences of each and every economic reorganization entailed by the growth process, in the endeavour to determine which, on balance, are beneficial and which are not. It may justly be protested that this is impracticable; that we cannot foretell the consequences, tangible and intangible, of the economic and social reorganizations resulting from a succession of interdependent technological innovations. However, we can make some attempt to sort things out. We may put aside until later some general reflections on certain potent albeit intangible factors, and in the meantime consider the sorts of welfare criteria by which economists have sought to justify the adoption of one policy as against alternative policies. The scope for such criteria is admittedly restricted, as we shall presently see, but the notions on which they are raised help to orient our thinking. Moreover, in circumstances where their application may be admitted, they can be very revealing. In particular, they enable us to point up some of the chief sources of 'ill-fare' that remain uncorrected under present institutions.

Indeed, we might go so far as to suggest that economic growth *per se* should be jettisoned as an independent goal of policy. For if we are concerned primarily with social welfare, those forms of economic growth that meet our welfare criteria will in any case be approved and adopted, the remainder being rejected: thus, sources of 'worthwhile' economic growth will continue to be sought after.

(2) A more equal distribution of real income has long been recognized by Western societies as one of the chief aims of economic policy. While, in general, any change in the pattern of prices – of goods and/or of productive services – makes some people better and others worse off, the most effective short run method for redistributing real income is the levying of highly progressive income taxes and capital taxes, while making freely available to all the greater number of services provided by the Government.

On the assumption that the structure of ability in the UK is more equally distributed than the structure of disposable incomes, the existing policies for expanding educational opportunities have long run effects in equalizing earning power. Since so much is already being done in Britain along these lines, it would be useful, before moving on, to take stock of our present position.

As Professor Titmuss has pointed out,[3] the official statistics available are unreliable in so many aspects that any conclusion about the trend of income distribution over the last two decades

3. R. M. Titmuss, *Income Distribution and Social Change* (Allen & Unwin, London, 1963).

must be treated with a degree of caution that effectively forbids any presumption one way or the other. The common impression that there is greater social and economic equality today than there was, say, in the thirties is formed from several developments. (*a*) The extension to every employed person since 1948 of national insurance and the provision of a national health service covering every person in the country. Today over 40 per cent of the Government's current expenditure is on social services, compared with about a quarter in 1920; and this over a period that has seen public expenditure increase from 20 per cent of the net national expenditure to something approaching 50 per cent. (*b*) A rise in the average standard of living since the war of about 45 per cent (in terms of disposable real income) – much of this economic gain taking tangible shape as a widespread ownership of consumer durables such as motor-cars, washing machines, television sets, refrigerators, vacuum cleaners, and the like. (*c*) The maintenance during the postwar period of a high level of employment with unusually good opportunities for unskilled and juvenile labour – an era that seems to be coming to a close. (*d*) A gradual extension to all social groups in the community of higher education over the last two decades. The student population today is running at about a quarter of a million compared with some sixty thousand before the war, and the numbers are expected to rise rapidly over the next decade.

For all that, existing inequality of wealth still appears quite striking. According to Professor Meade,[4] the top 1 per cent of income recipients in 1959 took about 12 per cent of the total national income; they also accounted for nearly 50 per cent of the country's total income from property. The top 5 per cent took about a quarter of the national income, and about two thirds of the total income from property. None the less, the inspiration towards a greater degree of equalization does not, or should not draw its strength only from a sense of unfairness, or envy on contemplating the figures at the top end of the scale. After all, one can envisage a society having a small proportion of very rich

4. J. E. Meade, *Efficiency, Equality and the Ownership of Property* (Allen & Unwin, London, 1964).

families, withal a comfortable standard of living for the remainder. This is not the condition in Britain, however. Despite the extension of welfare services and the increase in pensions and unemployment benefit since the war, the position at the lower end of the scale is anything but reassuring. The official income figures are not very helpful since the breakdown is by person and not by family, and many of the poor do not earn any income in the official sense. But we do know that in 1964–5, at any one time, some two million people were receiving support from the National Asistance Board, the bulk of them old age pensioners, to say nothing of an estimated 200,000 more who were eligible but who did not apply for assistance. Bearing in mind that the maximum earnings of a husband and wife receiving such assistance cannot be much more than £5 a week; bearing in mind further that, of the remainder of the six million pensioners (entitled to £3 7s. 6d. for a single person and £5 9s. 0d. for a married couple) many of them have little more than their pensions to live on; and, finally, comparing these figures with the average *per capita* earnings of the working population of about £18 a week,[5] one cannot escape the conclusion that a substantial degree of poverty and hardship for old people lingers on in the so-called welfare state of this affluent society.

In order to make a dent in this problem, a sum of the order of about half a billion pounds a year would have to be transferred to the underprivileged group – about 2 per cent of our national income. On the face of things, an income transfer of this magnitude is rather formidable, though not impracticable on economic grounds given the political will. Indeed, it is something less than the average annual increase of our national income. A reduction of our defence budget to about three quarters of the present estimate would suffice to provide it. If no reduction of government expenditure took place, however, it would require an addition in the first year of between two shillings and two-and-sixpence to the standard rate of income tax to raise the sum, though less

5. These figures are for 1964–5. Since 29 March 1966 the pension has been raised to £4 for a single person and £6 10s. for a married couple. Earnings *per capita* in 1965–6 were closer to £19 a week.

than this if capital gains were taxed at the same rate as income.

Putting this hard core poverty into a special category since, in the absence of direct concern by the State, it is not likely to disappear of itself over the foreseeable future, and turning to the remainder of the community, one might hazard the guess that the movement towards increasing equality will continue for some time as the advantages of being born into wealth are increasingly offset by the educational opportunities being opened to young people in every social and income group. The one major contingency that can upset these sanguine expectations is that of an unemployment crisis within the next few years caused by the rapid adoption of automation in industry and commerce.[6] Looking beyond such a crisis and farther into the future when such educational policies as we are now pursuing will have established a thorough-going meritocracy – one in which those born into talent (instead of wealth) will inherit top positions, and those found wanting will be relegated to the bottom of the social hierarchy – it cannot be foreseen whether disposable incomes and wealth will be more equally distributed than they are today. But there is no reason to suppose that the distributional structure of gross income, once it comes to reflect the distribution of native ability, will be any less unequal than it is under the existing system.

(3) Leaving out the problem of hard-core poverty in Britain, one should not expect any great accession of social welfare from attempts to accelerate the trend towards a more equal distribution of disposable income and wealth. In contrast, one may anticipate immediately perceptible benefits from the introduction of legislation to curb the chief sources of disamenity that afflict our daily lives. In order, however, to make a respectable economic case for such legislation, we need first to make explicit the notion of an ideal allocation of resources, with its implied criterion of social welfare. It will soon become apparent that social

6. Since there is a prevalent belief that technological innovation cannot cause unemployment, Appendix A is devoted to a cursory analysis of this possibility.

enterprise, working within the framework of current institutions at least has no tendency to bring about this ideal allocation.

Private enterprise, when working smoothly, does have the virtue of using variations in prices and outputs to match supplies to amounts demanded; the smoother it is working the faster are shortages and surpluses eliminated. The mechanism is simple: if a shortage appears in any good its price tends to rise, so acting to ration the limited supplies. But the profit of producing that good also rises, which brings about an expansion of its output and overcomes the initial shortage. If, on the other hand, there is a surplus of any good on the market, its price tends to fall, which induces increased consumption, while the profit on its production falls, which brings about a reduction of output thus eliminating the initial surplus. A good deal of so-called economic planning does no more than utilize methods for anticipating future excess demands and supplies in the various sectors of the economy, and, where necessary, take measures to reduce the consequent periods of maladjustment. This is an extremely useful task, yet a subsidiary one in so far, at least, as it is more desirable that the economy should move in the right direction – towards an ideal, or 'optimal' allocation – than that it should merely move more quickly and, possibly, in the wrong direction. At any rate, the principles on which an improvement in resource-allocation may be determined are logically prior to, and may be treated in separation from, the question of speed of adjustment. It will be simpler, therefore, if we put aside this speed-of-adjustment aspect of the problem, in order to focus attention on the allocation problem – on the 'optimal' set of outputs and prices; those towards which the economic system 'ought' to be tending at any moment.

The principle that a good should be produced if, and only if, its value to society exceeds its costs of production suggests that production of any good should be expanded until its value (which declines with the increase in output) is no longer greater than its 'marginal cost' – the addition to total cost incurred in producing one unit more of the good in question. The principle thus extended is commonly known as *marginal-cost pricing* since, if the units of output are small enough, the 'optimal' output is reached by producing to the point at which the market price is equal to marginal cost.

If the reader accepts the principle of marginal-cost pricing he may turn at once to Chapter Four which inquires into the nature of those non-commercial costs incurred in the process of production, or utilization, of certain kinds of goods. Once such additional costs are brought into the calculus, the production of apparently profitable items may have to be seriously curtailed. However, it is possible that readers, both general and specialized, are unconvinced of the rationale of marginal-cost pricing, at least of employing this allocation rule in any *partial* analysis – one restricted to a small segment of the economy in disregard of the relevant features in the rest of the economy. If so, a reading of the following digression purporting to outline the rationale of marginal-cost pricing, and the obstacle to its generality, may increase their receptivity to the arguments that follow.

Part Two

The Rationale
of Marginal-Cost Pricing

I

BEFORE talking about an improvement in the allocation of resources we require certain ethical premises on which judgements of better or worse are to be raised. In the West they have usually been of a libertarian character: nothing is good for society unless it is held to be good by the individuals who form that society. And while it is true that there are people who appear to be incompetent judges of their own interests, this is usually regarded as an argument for education rather than for paternalism. Be this as it may, since there is no providential method of determining the true interests of any persons which would command general assent, it would be impolitic at this early stage to premise propositions about social welfare on anything other than each man's view of his own interest. Though aware then of its occasional falsehood we follow, provisionally, the liberal convention of regarding each man as the best judge of his own welfare.

Let us define an improvement in the allocation of society's resources in a way familiar to economists – as an economic reorganization of those resources, involving a change in the collection of goods produced and in their distribution, which could make some people better off (in their own estimation) without making anyone else worse off. An 'optimal', or 'ideal', or 'summit' position – the adjectives are used interchangeably – is therefore defined as one from which no economic reorganization can qualify as an *improvement* in resource-allocation: in other words, an optimal position is one from which no economic reorganization is possible that makes some people better off without in the process making at least one person worse off. Alternatively, an optimal position may be interpreted as one that does not contain any 'slack', inasmuch as there is no way of reorganizing production and distribution as to make everyone better off than he is.

Such an optimal position of the economy has associated with it a well-known property: that the collection of finished goods valued at the prevailing prices has a higher value than that of any alternative collection of goods that could be produced with the existing resources of society. This property, is indeed, a corollary of the definition of an optimal position. For if it were otherwise, if one could reshuffle the existing resources so as to produce a collection of goods with a yet *greater* value at the initial prices, then it would, after all, be possible to give everyone the same value of goods as he enjoyed before and still have some goods left over. The value of these goods left over could then make one or more persons better off. But this implies that an allocative improvement is still possible. Therefore the so-called optimal position was not, after all, optimal as defined. It cannot then be otherwise than as stated: an optimal position has the property that, valued at its prevailing prices, no other collection of goods producible with the same total resources of society can be worth more than the optimal collection.

How can we know when the economy is at an optimal position? In general, when no resource – no type of labour, or of machinery, or of land – can be made to yield a higher value when transferred to some other employment. If we follow the custom of regarding these resources as divisible into very small units – an expository convenience – and also, to some extent, substitute for one another, this highest-value property of an optimal position, mentioned above, can be expressed by saying that the value contributed by a unit of any type of resource will be the same at the margin for all goods in which it is used. For example, in an optimal position, the value contributed by an additional, or marginal, unit of a given type of labour in textile production, in fishing, in barley cultivation, and in every other process in which it is used, must be the same. If it were otherwise: if it were still possible to transfer a resource from its current occupation to some other occupation in which the value of its contribution were larger, we should have succeeded in increasing total value at the prevailing set of prices. It would, therefore, follow from our first optimal property that we could not have been in an optimal position to start with. Hence the standard optimal rule, or allocation rule, that the marginal value contributed by any type of resource be the same in all its uses to which it can be put.

We may take a further step by supposing that the market functions well enough to set a single price for each type of resource. If now production is so organized that everywhere output is expanded to the point at which the marginal value contributed by any type of resource is equal to its price, the allocation rule must everywhere be met. For if in all uses the marginal value produced by any kind of resource is equal to its market-determined price then, clearly, this marginal value contributed by any type of resource must be the same in all uses. Hence, assuming a single market price for each type of resource, we may express the allocation rule as requiring that the marginal value of any resource be equal to its market price.[1]

It is necessary to recognize, at this stage, that by dividing both the marginal value contributed by a resource and the market price of that resource by the number of units of any good contributed by the marginal resource, the above allocation rule (that the marginal value of a resource must equal its price) is transformed into the rule that the price of the good be equal to its marginal cost. Thus we arrive at the common recommendation of marginal-cost pricing in industry as a means of establishing an optimal position.

There are, however, two complications we must face up to in connexion with marginal-cost pricing.

1. It is interesting to note in passing that a so-called perfectly competitive economy tends towards such an optional position. By definition of such an economy firms accept the market prices of all goods and of all resources as beyond their power to influence. Each firm will profitably expand so long as the value contributed by employing an additional resource of any kind exceeds the price of that resource. In equilibrium there is no incentive for additional firms to come in, or for expansion or contraction of existing firms. Each firm is, in fact, producing an output at which the marginal value of each resource is equal to its price. If all industries are organized in this way, the value of the marginal contribution of each type of resource is the same in all products, so establishing an optimal position.

The first has to do with the distribution of the national product, or the national income, among the members of society. We have shown that once an optimal position is reached the value of the goods is as high as or higher than the value of any other producible collection of goods *provided* we value all alternative collections of goods at the particular set of prices prevailing in the initially optimum position. But the relative prices of these goods arise, in principle, from the pattern of demand that emerges from the distribution of income associated with the collection of goods that is being produced in the optimal position in question. A change in individual tastes which changes the pattern of demand can obviously move the economy to a new optimal position. But, from what we have just said about distribution, there can also be a change to a new optimal position without any change in individual tastes taking place. For instance, any redistribution of income – arising, say, from alterations in taxation and government expenditures – may change the overall pattern of demand and, therefore (unless supply prices happen to remain everywhere constant irrespective of quantity produced), the set of prices also. If this happens, then the particular collection of goods that was previously optimal will not, in general, have the highest possible value at these new prices – though, as we have already shown, any *new* optimal collection of goods will certainly have this property. One may therefore assume, in general, that there is an indefinite number of optimal collections of goods that can be produced with the existing resources of the economy, each one generated by some particular income distribution and associated with a distinct set of product prices.

The neglect of this interconnexion between income-distribution and resource-allocation has been a potent source of confusion in the past. Notwithstanding all that has been written in recent years on this subject, unsophisticated writers venturing into the field of resource-allocation frequently argue as if these two considerations, distribution and allocation, can always be treated separately. Under certain conditions – constant costs in the production of all goods and services – the set of goods *prices* will be the same for any optimal position, each optimal position being distinguishable from the others only in containing a different collection of goods. Under other conditions yet more far-fetched – each person buying the same proportions of all goods as everyone else irrespective of his income – no conceivable distribution of income makes any difference to the resulting pattern of demand and, therefore, to the optimal collection of goods which, in these conditions, is uniquely determined. These are special cases, however, and though in the real world the universal-constant cost case may be important, as a general proposition it must be affirmed that an optimal position is optimal only for a given distribution; also the value of the optimal collection is a maximum only when valued at the resulting set of prices.

The second complication is the apparent all-or-nothing character of the applicability of the allocation rule. If for any reason we are unable to meet the allocation rule in each and every sector of the economy its application in the remaining sectors may not improve matters: thus, an adopted procedure of meeting the allocation rule whenever it can be met need not move us closer to an optimal position, and may even move us farther away from one. If, to illustrate, the output of the steel industry were such that all steel products were priced at twice their corresponding marginal costs and, for institutional reasons, this situation could not be altered, we should not be doing the best we can in the circumstances by strict marginal-cost pricing in the remaining sectors of the economy. In this simple case, as it happens, we do know what to do: we can come closest to an optimal position by adjusting the outputs of all other goods so that their prices also are twice as large as their corresponding marginal costs. This arrangement is, in fact, optimal since it ensures that the marginal value contributed by each type of resource is the same in all goods. However, in less simple cases – where, for example, several industries produce unalterable quantities of goods having quite different price–marginal cost ratios–the 'second best' allocation rules for the remainder of the economy are not easy to determine. Even where they could be determined they might be far too complex to be of any practical use.

II

Let us consider these two complications in a little more detail.

The interconnexion between resource-allocation and income-distribution seems to suggest, on the surface of things, that a bias in favour of the *status quo* enters whenever one aims to bring the economy closer to an optimum using the existing set of prices, since this set of prices itself emerged from the existing income-distribution. Unless we have special reasons to be satisfied with the existing distribution of income the optimal position corresponding to this existing set of prices has no more claim on our attentions than any other 'efficiently produced' collections of goods.[2] For each of these efficiently produced collections could be made optimal by some appropriate distribution of income. The only satisfactory solution to this problem seems to be that of choosing an optimum collection of goods which corresponds to some distribution of income that is, in some broadly accepted ethical sense, more satisfactory to the community than any other.

Suppose, however, that there are political limits to the degree of income redistribution that is feasible over the foreseeable future, must we waive any pronouncements about resource allocation? Not necessarily. The less we are able to alter, for institutional reasons, the existing structure of income distribution the more likely is it that all discernible movements towards any optimal position will be such that everyone is made better off. But even where the distributional structure of incomes is allowed to vary widely, it may turn out to be the case that the resulting pattern of demand, and, therefore, the optimal collection of goods, remains substantially unaltered. If the world were like that, we could quite logically pursue allocative improvements independently of their distributional effects, even though it may be ethically unacceptable to ignore these effects. If we did so in such circumstances, however, we would be enabled to say without ambiguity that gainers in a movement to an optimal position

2. An 'efficiently' produced collection of goods is one produced with existing resources and techniques and with such economy that it is not possible to produce more of any good without reducing the output of some other good.

could always fully compensate the losers and themselves be better off than they were in the existing non-optimal position.[3] Now if the gainers did *not* compensate the losers, the resulting distribution might well be worse than it was in the non-optimal position. We might then require either that no move towards optimality be made unless the resulting distribution was judged to be no worse, or else that losers be fully compensated in moving towards the optimal position. In the latter case nobody is actually made worse off and some are made better off. Since progressive taxes are a means of redistributing gains, the more highly progressive is the tax structure the more warrant there is for pursuing optimality without regard to distributional considerations. In the limiting case of taxation that equalized all incomes, any movement to an optimal position will actually make everyone better off.

Turning to the 'second best' problem which arises, say, when in several sectors of the economy there is no prospect of being able to enforce the allocation rule that outputs be adjusted to bring prices into equality with corresponding marginal costs, there is, as indicated, no simple and general rule to guide industrial outputs. But does this mean that there is no practical guidance available to the policy-maker concerned with improving allocation? Again, not necessarily, for if we had information to suggest that, after meeting the marginal cost pricing rule in all those sectors in which it could be met, the residual movement of resources that would yet be necessary to bring the unaccommodating sectors into line was slight, we could proceed to enforce the rule in all the accommodating sectors with a good conscience. By doing so we attain a position that is at least close to an optimal position. And for practical purposes this is very satisfactory.

3. In virtue of the definition of an optimum position we can already say that no movement from it, to any other position, is able to make everyone better off. What is more pertinent, however, to the idea of an allocative improvement is the stronger statement that in the movement from any non-optimal position to an optimal position everyone could be made better off (alternatively, some could be made better off and no one worse off) – that is, gainers could more than compensate losers. And this statement, as indicated above, is true only in special cases.

True, we know that there exists some conceivable reshuffling of resources that would enable us, if we could discover it, to reach yet a higher position – the elusive second-best position itself. But we also know that the margin of hypothetical gain is narrow.

Again, if several of the alterable sectors are severely out of line with all the other sectors – say prices in these alterable sectors are far below their corresponding marginal costs compared with all other sectors – we may almost certainly improve the situation by operating on these several sectors alone. For a contraction of the outputs of these several sectors, to the point at which their price–marginal cost ratios increased to the extent necessary to equal the *average* ratio of the remaining sectors of the economy (without increasing the spread of these ratios among these remaining sectors) would effectively narrow the spread of price–marginal cost ratios for the whole economy. The new position would then be closer to an optimum than it was before we reduced the outputs of these several low ratio sectors. In general, the further is price in one sector below its marginal cost compared with the range of price–marginal cost ratios in the remaining sectors, the more sure one can be that the gain from transferring units of resource from this sector to the others – a movement of resources towards sectors in which their value is higher – will overcome any countervailing repercussions on other prices.

This same argument may carry more conviction if put differently. Starting from a non-optimal position we count as an improvement any economic reorganization that enables everyone to be made better off unambiguously. If we effect some reduction of output in, say, the automobile industry, which alteration would enable us to make unambiguously better off all those people directly concerned with automobiles – the producers, employees, purchasers, and all those affected by the manner of producing and utilizing automobiles – the definition of an improvement has been met *provided* that people not directly concerned with automobiles remain relatively unaffected. This condition is met if in the remainder of the economy (the R sector) there are negligible changes in the prices of goods and resources in consequence of the reduction of output in the automobile sector (the A sector). The less likely is this latter condition to be met, however, the more important is it that the repercussions in the R sector be taken into account before attempting to strike a balance of gain or loss. Thus the crucial assumption which, if met, would justify the partial approach followed in the next few chapters is that the gains from curtailing output in any A sector are large relative to the repercussions in the R sector. For the discussion of the disamenities inflicted on society by motorized traffic I shall be assuming this condition is easily met.[4]

4. This same condition permits us, if we wish, to ignore or to treat separately any incidental benefits conferred on society by economic activity. I happen to believe that such benefits or 'external economies' that remain to be exploited are of limited significance and, therefore, that there is little social welfare to be gained by prescribing for them. None the less, an attachment to the contrary opinion need not prevent any reader from agreeing with my arguments. If net external *diseconomies* are large and un-corrected, an increase in social welfare follows their correction whether or not there are, in other industries, external economies remaining to be properly exploited.

4

The Nature of External Diseconomies

IN this and the remaining chapters in Part II we shall concern ourselves closely with the implications for social welfare of those 'neighbourhood effects' generated by a wide range of economic activities. The operations of firms, or the doings of ordinary people, frequently have significant effects on others of which no account need be taken by the firms, or the individuals, responsible for them. Moreover, inasmuch as the benefits conferred and the damages inflicted – or 'external economies' and 'external diseconomies' respectively – on other members of society in the process of producing, or using, certain goods do not enter the calculation of the market price, one can no longer take it for granted that the market price of a good is an index of its marginal value to society.[1]

If there are external diseconomies being generated either in the process of production of certain goods, or in their final use by the public, damages are being inflicted on other people to which some value may be attached. It follows that the *social* value of a good – the value remaining after subtracting from its market

1. In the absence of all neighbourhood effects the changes of tastes and of techniques of production would cause changes in product and factor prices over time, and therefore changes in the distribution of income. Nobody engaged in private industry is concerned with the ultimate effects of his activity on the distribution of income, although of course each person is subject to some risk that the market will go against him. Yet even if we supposed everyone to be indifferent to the resulting pattern of distribution, a concern with allocative efficiency implies a concern with neighbourhood effects. Uncorrected external diseconomies in certain sectors of the economy, for instance, would indicate that a position in which everywhere price was equal to marginal cost was not in fact optional. By correcting these external diseconomies an optimal position, one in which everyone could be made better off, is attainable.

price the estimated value of the damage inflicted on others by producing and/or using the good – may not only be well below its market price, it may even be negative. In such cases we are required to reduce outputs until this social value of the good is raised sufficiently to become equal to its marginal cost of production. Alternatively, we may leave the market price uncorrected and instead transform the *private* marginal cost, calculable by the producer on strict commercial principles, into *social* marginal cost by adding to the private marginal cost the value of any incidental damage inflicted on the rest of society in the production, or final use, of the good in question.[2] When this correction is applied to each unit of any relevant output, the universal *private* marginal-cost pricing rule becomes amended to the more general *social* marginal-cost pricing rule. It follows that an apparently efficiently working competitive economy, one in which outputs are quickly adjusted so that prices everywhere tend to equal *private* marginal cost, may lead the economy very far indeed from an optimal position as defined. Such an optimal position in fact requires that in all sectors production be such that prices are equal to social marginal cost.

Although the principle is straightforward enough such estimates of damages (and benefits) can pose considerable practical difficulties. One reason for this, as we shall see, is that some sorts of external diseconomies, manifestly important ones at that, do not lend themselves easily to measurement – no small defect in a society so prone as ours is to equate relevance with quantification. Another reason is that, even though measurable, their incidence may be so widely dispersed that adequate data are difficult to procure. Furthermore, there may be difficulties both of concept and measurement in attributing to any single sector of the economy a variety of external diseconomies which depend for their effect upon complementary economic activities. The smoky factory chimney is a favourite example simply because it appears to limit itself so conveniently to spreading dirt

2. It should be obvious that the value of any benefit conferred on society by the good in question is to be subtracted from its private marginal cost.

within a locality; the additional costs of keeping one's person and one's clothes clean in the polluted areas can easily be estimated and added to the private costs in order to yield an estimate of the social costs of production. The costs of water pollution by one or more factories is also amenable to calculation of this sort since the authorities usually have estimates of the damages being caused and of the higher costs of alternative sources of pure water. Some of the simpler nuisances, on the other hand, such as excessive engine noise and emission of noxious fumes, may be tackled most economically by enacting compulsory noise-muffling measures and compulsory installation of anti-fume devices, as in several states of the US. However, more general social afflictions such as industrial noise, dirt, stench, ugliness, urban sprawl, and other features that jar the nerves and impair the health of many are difficult both to measure and to impute to any single source – which is, of course, no reason for treating them with resignation.

One must insert a caveat at this juncture, however. The detection of some uncorrected external effect does not of itself warrant government intervention. First the external diseconomy that acts to reduce the social marginal cost and suggests a reduction of output may be generated by a highly monopolistic industry which, in the absence of the external diseconomy, would require expansion of output. In general it is the balance of these two features that determines the change of output. In fact we are concerned only with those external diseconomies so large as to be obviously in need of remedial correction. Secondly, it is possible that the affected groups will come to agreement by themselves, or with a little official encouragement, an event that is more likely to take place if the parties that suffer the damage are well organized, as are firms and industries, than if they comprise a host of individuals with no mutual connexions, or interests in common, other than this. Thirdly, and if they do not reach any voluntary agreement, the cost of intervening and administering a satisfactory scheme may exceed the apparent social gain. Nevertheless, by concentrating in the following chapters on the more blatant examples of external diseconomies imposed on the public at large by modern industries we shall not need to invoke this caveat.

The growing incidence of the external diseconomies generated by certain sectors of the economy and suffered by the public at large, regarded as the most salient factor responsible for the misallocation of our national resources, is one of the chief themes of this essay and the motif of this second part of the volume. All professional economists are, of course, aware of the role played by external diseconomies[3] in the system; though, alas, all too many of them tend to look at such effects merely as one of the chief obstacles to facile theorizing – as the sort of possibility that detracts from the optimal properties of the popular theoretical construct, a perfectly competitive economy – rather than as an existing social menace. Familiarity with so simple a concept, and ritual footnote references to it, seem to have imparted a feeling that the matter is well under control. Too many economists have, therefore, continued to ignore the events taking shape around them and to immerse themselves instead in the intellectual fascination of quasi-mathematical models of growth, and the theoretical problems involved in general solutions of optimal systems.

Not that the damage wrought by external diseconomies is entirely ignored by the public at large. Apart from letters of protest and occasional newspaper comment, magazines such as *Punch* and the *New Yorker* which specialize in social satire frequently depict with biting humour the dilemmas of automobilization, and the frustration of the millions all trying simultaneously to get away to a quiet place. But this does not meet the problem since, if anything, this laughing at the follies of mankind serves to release social tension and makes bearable what in fact ought not to be borne with. If the problem is to be tackled by society, the economist must persist in revealing the nature of the beast, and must suggest the circumstances under which meaningful magnitudes may be attributed to external effects. Nor should

3. As indicated in the footnote on page 81, the implications of external diseconomies may, under the conditions stated, be treated separately from those of external economies.

he shirk detailed description of cases wherever the social consequences that escape the pricing system appear to be so involved that a comprehensive criterion for evaluating them cannot, as yet, be satisfactorily evolved.

5

External Diseconomies and
Property Rights (i)

I

TOWARDS the end of the preceding chapter we disclosed the nature of those significant external diseconomies that cause social marginal costs of some goods to exceed their corresponding private marginal costs (or, expressed otherwise, that cause the social value of certain goods to fall below their market price). Let us begin from a situation in which outputs are already determined by the private marginal-cost rule. In order to correct a misallocation of resources resulting from external diseconomies, and thus to attain an optimal position, we are required in general[1] to reduce production of all goods in which the process of manufacture, or use, generates conspicuous external diseconomies. A method alternative to that of direct government intervention in reducing the production levels of the relevant sectors in the economy, and one which has intuitive appeal, is to bring about a reduction in the output of the damaging industry, by compelling it to pay out, for each unit produced, an amount necessary to compensate those members of society for damages suffered in consequence of the production, or use, of each unit produced. Such a correction, by adding to the commercial cost of each item produced a compensatory sum, transforms the industry's schedule of private marginal cost into one of social marginal cost. Should the method be adopted, however, and the resultant

1. By attributing an external diseconomy directly to a single input, and by making the unusual assumption that as output of a good is increased *less* of this input is required, we can concoct an instance in which taxing, or otherwise reducing, the output of a good takes one further from an optimal position. (See C. R. Plott, 'Externalities and Corrective Taxes', *Economica*, 1966.) The external diseconomies considered here are all generated, we suppose, from the process of combining inputs, or the process of using the finished good.

costs of production to the industry raised, not only would the output of the damaging industry be reduced (to the point, if it exists, at which this social marginal cost of output, which now includes compensation, is covered by the market price) it would also transfer income to the injured parties. Enforced compensation then would cause not only an allocative effect – a shift of resources away from the production of goods generating external diseconomies – but also a distribution effect: a transfer of money to the victims of damage from those inflicting it.

Now one may presume to discern in this proposal for compensation either (1) an unsolvable problem, as it does not require much philosophy to detect in such external diseconomy situations a divergence of interest between two groups, or (2) no problem at all since the damages sustained by one group provide an incentive to come to an agreement with the other group. Let us illustrate these two views using the familiar example of a small town factory producing vacuum cleaners, the volume of whose output is guided by the private marginal-cost rule but whose chimneys foul the air in the surrounding residential areas. Suppose a survey were made of the claims for damages by the inhabitants, these being largely the costs of extra laundering charges and extra soap, and the total amount presented to the factory-owner for payment. If the factory-owner were required to pay this bill or else to agree to installing anti-smoke devices, he might well complain that such an arrangement, though it met the claims of the inhabitants, did so only by damaging his own interests. Indeed, he might argue that if, for instance, he elected to install anti-smoke devices he ought to be compensated for the loss of profit incurred by their installation. Were it cheaper instead to give satisfaction to claimants by reducing his output somewhat, and therefore his profits also, he would again consider himself justified in demanding compensation.

As it happens the amount by which he has to reduce his output in pursuit of the *social* marginal cost rule is exactly the same whether he compensates the inhabitants for the damage they suffer from his smoky chimneys or whether instead he is compensated by them for reducing his output and therefore his profits.[2] To illustrate, suppose that the damage suffered by the inhabitants varies directly with the output of vacuum cleaners that the manufacturer produces, he would have to add to the marginal cost of each vacuum cleaner produced a sum equal, say, to £5 more to cover the cost of the damage. Raising his price accordingly reduces the demand for his vacuum cleaners by, let us say, 40 per cent. This reduced output, at which social marginal cost is now equal to the new price, becomes his most profitable output (*additional* units could only be sold at a price below this social marginal cost, while the production of *fewer* units, to be sold at a price above social marginal cost, implies that he forgoes potential profit). On the other hand, were he not compelled by law to pay damages the inhabitants might come together and agree to bribe him to reduce his output. The maximum bribe they could afford, by reference to the soap and laundering expenses incurred in meeting the smoke damage caused in the production of each additional vacuum cleaner, is of course equal to £5 per unit, the amount they would otherwise have to bear. By offering him this much in compensation for each vacuum cleaner less he produced they would induce him to reduce his output by exactly 40 per cent, and no more. For beyond a 40 per cent reduction of output the gross profit per vacuum cleaner – which profit rises with the price as output is reduced – becomes greater than the payment of £5 which is the maximum compensation the inhabitants can offer.

In such cases, from a purely allocative point of view, the correct or optimal output is attained irrespective of which party compensates the other. The question of who *ought* to compensate has therefore to be settled on other grounds. This illustration may also seem to lend support to proposition (2), that such problems tend to be self-correcting, since it is clearly in the interests of the inhabitants themselves to agree voluntarily to

2. Whenever the value of the damages can be agreed upon by reference to market prices (here costs of laundering and soap, etc.) the reduction of output necessary to meet the social marginal cost rule may be uniquely determined irrespective of who is compensating whom. If not, if the damage has to be subjectively evaluated – without reference to market prices – then the 'optimal output' will in general differ according to who compensates whom.

offer him compensation so as to reduce smoke damage, whether the factory-owner chooses to do so by reducing his output or by installing anti-smoke devices.

Before reviewing these arguments (1) and (2) critically, however, we must bear in mind the nature of the improvement involved in a movement to an optimal output. In a partial economic setting, such as that exemplified by the factory whose smoky chimneys impose extra costs on the local inhabitants, we should be able to disregard as negligible all price movements in the economy save those under direct scrutiny. In such a setting, one in which all prices other than those of these vacuum cleaners remain unchanged, a movement towards the optimal output – a contraction in the annual output of vacuum cleaners in this example – can be identified as one in which everyone involved *could* be made better off. Thus beginning from the uncorrected volume of output, each additional reduction by a unit of output that brings us closer to the optimal output contributes some *net* social gain. This is because (1) the gain, equal to the *reduction* of social damages, estimated at £5 for each additional vacuum cleaner produced, exceeds (2) the loss of commercial profit per unit vacuum cleaner, which profit increases to £5 per vacuum cleaner only when output has been reduced by 40 per cent. These net social gains *could* then be distributed as to make all parties better off than they were in the uncorrected market situation.

All this is but an attempt at popular exposition of common doctrine, but in order to make intelligent use of this social marginal-cost rule as a means of reaching an optimal output we must recognize the influence of the existing institutional framework on the market solution. Indeed, any concern with (A) the distribution of wealth, (B) the incentive towards promoting improved allocation, and (C) equity or justice, must have regard to the key role played by institutional arrangements.

II

(A) Under the heading of distribution, two kinds of situations must be distinguished: (*a*) the first is that brought out in our smoky chimney example in which the optimal output is *uniquely determined* irrespective of whether the factory-owner is made to reduce his output by being legally compelled to compensate the inhabitants for the damage they suffer, or whether, instead, the inhabitants agree to compensate the factory-owner for each unit of output he forbears to produce. Whichever party compensates the other the movement to an optimal output is such as to enable everyone to be made better off there than he was in the uncorrected market situation. But even if the optimal output was reached while *actually* making everyone better off than he was in the uncorrected market situation – say, by having the inhabitants come together and bribe the factory-owner for each unit of output reduced, or to compensate him for the cost of installing smokeless chimneys – we might well feel dissatisfied with the result. After all, the factory-owner may be rich and the inhabitants poor. A more progressive distribution of income would result – and, of course, the same optimal output reached – if the factory-owner were, instead, compelled to pay the inhabitants full damages for each vacuum cleaner he produced (or else be compelled to install smokeless chimneys at his own expense). As it stands, however, the law may well favour the factory-owner who need take no account of the damages he inflicts on others in pursuit of profits and 'progress'. If so, he is then in a position to be made still better off if those who suffer damages at his hand have no recourse but to bribe him to restrain his activities: for the compensation offered him to reduce the initial units of output is likely to exceed the profit per unit he sacrifices.

(*b*) The second kind of situation is that in which the optimal situation is not uniquely determined but itself depends upon the distribution of income as between the opposing parties.[3] Let us

3. Another way in which income distribution influences optimal positions has been briefly described in the preceding chapter. There it was shown how a change in the distribution of incomes could lead of itself to a new optimal

illustrate this possibility with an example of a person B having a legal right, and wishing to build a house in a location that obscures the view of the surrounding countryside currently enjoyed by A. A, being richer than B, is willing to pay a maximum sum, say £2,000, rather than have a newcomer, B, build on the site in question, a sum which exceeds the minimum amount, say £500, that B agrees to accept in order to seek another site. The existing situation, with A's view unobscured by B's house, is optimal according to the accepted definition. For it is not possible to adopt the alternative situation and make both A and B better off. (Indeed, if B initially decided to build there he could easily be bribed by A not to build there, so that both A and B would be better off in comparison with a new situation in which B just went ahead, built his house, and obscured A's view.)

Now suppose instead that the new arrival B is richer than A and is therefore willing to pay a maximum of up to £1,500 to A for permission to build his house there, a sum which exceeds the minimum sum, say £1,000, acceptable to A as compensation for his loss of view. The change to a situation in which B builds his house where he wishes now becomes a movement to an optimal position. For A and B can always strike a bargain in which the building of B's house makes them both better off compared with a situation in which B's house is not built. Indeed, if, as we suppose, B has planning permission to build his house where he pleases, A cannot bribe him to withdraw. The new situation, with B's house built to mar A's view, is now the optimal situation. As distinct, therefore, from the smoky chimney case, where the value of the damages inflicted is, we suppose, 'objectively' measurable by market prices (costs of extra soap, laundry, etc.), there is no unique optimal outcome. The optimal

---

solution with a different set of relative prices in the economy as a whole.

The phenomenon being discussed above is quite distinct, however. Here we focus on a small segment of the economy and disregard as negligible all price changes other than those operating within this segment. The issue now is the value to each of the contending parties of having its own way. And it will transpire that the richer is one party compared with the other, the more likely will the optimal solution coincide with his own interest.

outcome depends *inter alia* on the intial distribution of wealth as between the two contending parties A and B. If A is richer, the *status quo* is likely to be optimal. If B is richer, the situation favoured by B is likely to be optimal.

What is more, there may be instances in which the comparative wealth of the two parties is such that neither the *status quo* nor the movement from it can make both parties better off. Whichever of the alternative situations happens to be in existence appears, by definition, to be the optimal one. To illustrate, if A is prepared to pay a maximum of £1,000 to resist B's demands for the site in question, he may yet refuse to yield the site for a sum less than £1,200.[4] B, for his part, we may suppose, is willing to pay up to £1,100 for the site, though if it were his by right he would not surrender his claim to it for less than £1,300. The existing situation – one in which B's maximum of £1,100 does not suffice to bribe A, who will accept nothing less than £1,200 – is the optimal one since, by definition, a movement from it cannot make both A and B better off. If, however, the law gave B the right to build his house where he pleases, and in availing himself of that right B decides, after all, to build his house so as to obscure A's view, the new position is again optimal. A's maximum of £1,000 will not suffice to bribe B, who will not give up his right for less than £1,300. Both, that is, cannot be made better off by the change, and the new situation with B's house obscuring A's view is optimal. Unless we are content to let the optimal outcome vary with the law we shall have to invoke other criteria such as those involving equity, and discussed under (c) below.

---

4. From the proposition of the diminishing marginal utility of money income (where money income in such cases is assumed to be able to buy all goods other than that under consideration here at fixed prices) it follows that an addition of £1,000 to a man's income adds a smaller amount to his total utility than a subtraction of £1,000 removes from his total utility.

Hence, the minimum sum he is ready to accept to forgo a certain claim (a sum that is *added* to his income) must be larger than the maximum he will pay to implement his claim (a sum that is *subtracted* from his income) – the actual amount of utility, or real benefit, being of course the same, whether added to or subtracted from his real income.

Other examples of such cases could be given, all of them having the characteristic that the potential damage suffered by each of the contending groups cannot be uniquely valued by reference to market prices but instead is subjectively determined and, therefore, in general differs as between the contending parties. A and B could, for instance, be non-smoker and smoker sharing a room or, respectively, a group of residents in a secluded area and the promoter of a motor highway through that area, or more generally, those opposing and those supporting an urban development scheme. In all such cases, the wealthier the party the more likely is it that his, or its, favoured outcome will be the optimal outcome – though whether, in such cases, wealth is actually transferred from the wealthier party to the other in realizing this optimal outcome depends on the existing law.

III

(B) In a world in which costs (i) of enforcing the new economic arrangements between opposing interests, (ii) of acquiring all the information relevant to the external diseconomy in question, and (iii) of decision taking within any group, were all zero, it would follow that uncorrected external diseconomies, once recognized, would disappear. According to the provisions of the existing law either direct measures would be undertaken to adjust all relevant outputs according to the social marginal-cost rule or an optimal output (or outcome) would be voluntarily realized. Where, for example, there is no law to compel the factory-owner to install anti-smoke devices, or to compensate the victims of his enterprise, it would yet be in the interest of the inhabitants to agree among themselves (costlessly as we are supposing) to offer to compensate the factory-owner for each unit of output reduced. By such an offer the reduction towards the optimal output (a reduction beyond which output the social cost of the damage would be smaller than the profit sacrificed) is secured by voluntary means. We may not agree with the resulting distribution of wealth arising from such voluntary agreements, nor with the equity of the outcome. Nevertheless, in the complete absence of all such costs, the existence of external diseconomies would not require government intervention in order to bring about an ideal allocation of resources.

It is the fact that such costs are positive, however, that prevents the attainment of optimal positions. It might then seem valid to argue that if the 'virtual' optimal outcome (that which would be determined in the absence of all such costs) could not be reached simply because such costs were prohibitive the existing situation must, for all practical purposes, be optimal. But comforting as this sort of reasoning is to the *laissez-faire* proponents, the costs that prohibit voluntary agreement between parties are, in general, neither essential nor irreducible. Such costs, in fact, also depend upon the existing legal framework. If in the smoky chimney case there were no law to protect the interests of the inhabitants, it is most unlikely that voluntary agreement would be reached. Even if the initiative were there, the total costs of organizing a large dispersed heterogeneous group for the purpose of reaching agreement on the amount of compensation to the manufacturer and on the contribution of each of the affected inhabitants to this compensation would be very high. The costs of government initiative and administration are likely to be smaller, and if small enough there will remain a net gain from the movement to an optimal output.

Of greater interest yet, if the law were on the side of the victims of industrial damage, the difficulties of reaching voluntary agreement might be much smaller. The factory-owner, or the board of directors, can be depended upon to reach a decision pretty smartly when their material interests are threatened. If the law goes against them, they must weigh up the respective costs of installing smokeless chimneys, on the one hand, and of operating a scheme for compensating the victims, on the other. One concludes that the operation of the market – when the term is extended to include voluntary agreements reached about the methods for dealing with external diseconomies – is able to deal with such phenomena more satisfactorily within a certain legal framework, one that puts the burden of searching for agreement on the party that can reach and implement decisions with the least expense.

In the case of industry-generated external diseconomies, that party is the firm or firms comprising the industry. Even if we suppose that the industry chooses the method of compensating victims to that of removing the diseconomy, and also that the cost of (ii), the collecting of information of relevant damages sustained, is no less for the industry than for the public, the costs of (iii), decision taking, are incomparably lower for an industry than for a host of scattered individuals.

IV

(c) Finally, there is the question of the justice, or equity, of any existing legal framework which, as we have seen, incidentally encourages or discourages optimal adjustments. In comparing alternative economic situations certain dual welfare criteria have been proposed by economists; for instance, it is agreed to regard a situation II as superior to I if, first, II is allocatively superior (everyone in II *could* be made better off then he was in I), and second, if the distribution of income accompanying the II situation is, in some sense, better than that in I. Provided that such a dual criterion is consistent in itself [5] it may be employed exclusively where there are no other relevant considerations. But for the significant external diseconomies we are discussing in this essay there do happen to be other important considerations relating to equity. To touch on a trivial example first, let A, a non-smoker, and B, a smoker, share a room together. If the law prohibited smoking in the absence of unanimous consent, and B cannot bribe A to allow him to smoke, the no-smoking rule is optimal. If, on the other hand, the law does permit smoking, and so favours B's interest, the optimal situation may then be brought about;

5. Generally such a dual criterion will be internally consistent – that is, incapable in application of leading to contradictory results – if the allocative improvement is brought about by voluntary agreement between the affected parties. In such cases the change to an optimal position is such that it actually does make some people better off and no one worse off. (Such movements in which compensation is actually paid to induce one of the groups to agree to the improvement involve what is sometimes referred to as 'the principle of compensated adjustment'.)

voluntarily, by A's bribing B not to smoke. The latter event meets the dual criterion if A is the wealthier of the two, but for all that the arrangement may be held to be unsatisfactory. Some people might feel, for instance, that B should not in any event be pre-mitted to spoil the fresh air breathed by A. It may be urged that, even though he can afford to do so (which possibility suffices to make the no-smoking solution optimal), A should not have to bribe B to stop smoking.

Differences of opinion about compelling the party who is able to compensate the other actually to compensate him would be much smaller in other cases, say if B were using a new weeding machine that could not help blowing the weeds plucked from B's garden into A's garden. It is not likely that many people would agree to settle the question of compensation, if necessary, by reference to the disparity of income between them. We should then be more inclined to require that B compensate A for spoiling his garden. If A were poor enough, the optimal outcome might well be that B continue to use his new weeding machine. Since the value of his gain by using his weeding machine exceeds A's loss, an allocative improvement is thereby achieved. However, considerations not only of distribution (which meet the dual criterion), but of equity also, would require that A be fully compensated by B. If, on the other hand, A, whose garden suffers from B's weeding machine, were sufficiently richer than B, the optimal outcome would require that B desist from weeding his garden with the new machine. And though the other part of the dual criterion, *based on distribution alone*, would appear to require that B, the poorer party, be compensated, considerations of equity might now operate to forbid the payment of compensation to B. Thus although an optimal outcome may come about through actual compensatory payments irrespective of the law, *provided the costs of voluntary agreement are low enough*, any out-come that involves the payment of compensation to the party responsible for the disamenity – even though such party be the poorer of the two – may be ethically unacceptable.

6

External Diseconomies
and Property Rights (ii)

THE three considerations discussed in the preceding chapter, the existing distribution of wealth, the incentives to improved allocation within the existing institutional framework, and the justice or equity of that framework, combine to reveal the deficiencies of the *status quo*, in particular its inability to respond properly to significant external diseconomies. Suppose a private airport is to be built, or expanded, close enough to a large residential area as to disturb the peace of the inhabitants. In order to simplify the issues we may suppose that a fixed number of flights are involved all of which, if the airport is to be profitable, must be undertaken. The optimal outcome is, therefore, either that of siting the airport near this residential area or that of not siting it there. We may dismiss the simplest *laissez faire* argument that all is well, that an optimal outcome must be realized since either (1) the inhabitants are able to compensate the airport authorities to move elsewhere, and if so it will be in their own interests to bring this about, or else (2) they are unable to compensate the airport authorities, in which case the establishment of the airport is the optimal outcome. This argument, as we have seen, neglects the problem of initiative in organizing the protest, and it ignores the time, effort and money spent by large numbers of people in deciding not only the largest sum they can collectively offer but also the contribution to be made by each family. The larger the population affected the smaller is the likelihood of effective initiative and the higher the sum of the costs in reaching a decision. As suggested, however, these are not inevitable obstacles. If the existing law were such that the airport authorities were compelled to compensate the inhabitants, the costs of reaching a decision would be likely to be very much lower.[1] Even if these

1. Since we are concerned here to illustrate principles not to offer practical

costs were nil, however, it is altogether possible that the airport authorities could not afford to compensate the inhabitants. The optimal outcome would then require their plans to be changed: the airport would have to be sited elsewhere.

Again, there is the consideration that the individual resident families are poorer than the airport-owners, from which two things follow: first, the simple point that if we are interested in a more equal distribution of income and/or social justice, then in the event that the airport company *could* compensate all the victims of aircraft noise – implying by definition, that the siting of the airport there is the optimal outcome – we should require that the company actually compensate the victims. Secondly, in consequence of *subjective* (non-market) estimates of damages sustained by one or both of the opposing parties the optimal outcome may very easily be ambiguous even if we ignore all costs of reaching voluntary agreements and of implementing them. The *maximum* that any of the inhabitants is prepared to pay to the airport company to avoid aircraft noise is limited by his wealth, by his prospective income and assets. No matter how excruciating his suffering will be, his contribution is perforce limited. The *minimum* sum that he is willing to accept to bear with the aircraft noise is not, however, subject to such constraint. In fact such a sum will exceed the maximum he is prepared to pay by a margin that is wider the larger is the sum of money required to present him with feasible alternatives.[2] And the

---

proposals, we shall assume that all parties affected by the siting of the airport have the relevant knowledge on which to estimate their potential compensation payments, and, moreoover, that they consistently tell the truth. The costs of collecting information about compensation payments, and any costs of enforcing the optimal arrangements – costs (i) and (ii) – we continue to assume the same whichever party is to be compensated.

2. An extreme case of a man in the desert dying of thirst brings out this point convincingly. The maximum he would pay for a bucket of drinking water which would ensure his survival is limited by his prospective wealth. He could sign the lot away, but no more. The minimum sum he would be willing to take instead of the bucket of water – assuming he wished to live and was not stupid – would approach infinity; or rather, there could be no sum large enough to induce him to part with the life-saving bucket of water.

relevant alternative is not the sum that would suffice to soundproof his house – or suffice to soundproof a room of his house, as the government is apt to think – unless he is indifferent to being shut in his house all the year round. Indeed such a sum should not be less than the amount necessary to compensate him fully for the inconvenience and expense of moving to a quiet area similar in other respects. And if alternative quiet areas have disappeared so that it is not worth his while to move house, the minimal compensation that would enable him to feel no worse off than he was before being exposed to aircraft noise would be larger than this.[3] Thus, if we reckon the maximum sum that the inhabitants could pay to be rid of aircraft disturbance as £10 million, and the minimum they would be prepared to accept to bear with it is £20 million, and compare these figures with the sum, say, of £15 million which is the most the company is willing to pay to operate on this site, and, also, the least it will accept to move elsewhere – this £15 million being the capital value of the estimate of their excess future profits from operating on the

---

For in the circumstances, a sum of money, no matter how large, would be worth nothing to him since there are no alternative means at any price of keeping himself alive. Only as such means become available at a price does this minimum sum become finite.

3. The reader may now appreciate how recent calculations of the differences in the market value between houses, alike in all other relevant respects, at different distances from an airport, understate the loss suffered from aircraft noise for two reasons, (1) they represent an estimate of the maximum loss that house-owners in the noisier area are able and willing to bear to move out of the area; not the larger estimate of the minimum sum they would accept to put up with the noise. And, as alternative quiet zones become harder to find, this minimum sum they would accept grows relative to the maximum loss they are able and willing to bear. Indeed, even if there were several currently quiet areas into which a family might move, the lack of any announced government plan of maintaining noise-free zones leaves open a risk that effectively reduces the attraction of these areas. (2) If the Government's existing policy continues and noise-free inhabitable areas gradually disappear, an increased level of noise throughout the country as a whole is accompanied by a narrowing of differentials between areas. To regard such a calculation as an index of disamenity is absurd, since it will ultimately reveal zero disamenity for any area whenever all areas are subject to the same amount of aerial disturbance, no matter how great.

present site over the next best alternative site – the company could not be bribed by the inhabitants to move their airport elsewhere. Even if costs (i), (ii) and (iii) are all zero, then the decision already taken to establish the airport is the optimal one. If, on the other hand, the law found in favour of the inhabitants (and all costs again were zero) the company would be unable to compensate the inhabitants to put up with the disturbance. Once again, then, whichever situation the law brings about is the optimal one. Considerations both of the distribution of wealth and of plain justice, however, suggest that the victims of aircraft disturbance be given legal rights to full compensation.

In so far as the activities of private or public industry are in question, the alteration required of the existing law is clear. For private industry, when it bothers at all to justify its existence to society, is prone to do so just on the grounds that the value of what it produces exceeds the cost it incurs – gains exceed losses, in other words. But what are costs under the existing law and what ought to count as costs is just what is in issue. A great impetus would doubtless take place in the expansion of certain industries if they were allowed freely to appropriate or trespass on the land or properties of others. Even where they were effectively bought off by the victims, the owners of such favoured industries would thereby become the richer. And one could be sure that if, after the elapse of some years, the Government sought to revoke this licence there would be an outcry that such arbitrary infringement of liberties would inevitably 'stifle progress', 'jeopardize employment' and, of course, 'lose us valuable export markets'. Such an example though admittedly far-fetched is distinctly relevant. For private property in this country has been regarded as inviolate for centuries. Even if the Government during a national emergency or in pursuit of national policy takes over the ownership or management of private property it is obliged to compensate owners. It may well be alleged that in any instance the Government paid too little or too much, but it would not occur to a British Government merely to confiscate private property.

In extending this principle of compensation, largely on the

grounds of equity, the law should explicitly recognize also the facts of allocation. Privacy and quiet and clean air are scarce goods – far scarcer than they were before the war – and sure to become scarcer still in the foreseeable future. They are becoming more highly valued by millions of people, most of them anxious to find a quiet place to live not too far from their work. There is no warrant, therefore, for allowing them to be treated as though they were free goods, as though they were so abundant that a bit more or less made not the slightest difference to anyone. Clearly if the world were so fashioned that clean air and quiet took on a physically identifiable form, and one that allowed it to be transferred as between people, we should be able to observe whether a man's quantum of the stuff had been appropriated, or damaged, and institute legal proceedings accordingly. The fact that the universe has not been so accommodating in this respect does not in the least detract from the principle of justice involved, or from the principle of economy regarding the allocation of scarce resources. One has but to imagine a country in which men were invested by law with property rights in privacy, quiet, and in clean air – simple things, but for many indispensable to the enjoyment of life – to recognize that the extent of the compensatory payments that would perforce accompany the operation of industries, motorized traffic, and airlines would constrain many of them to close down or to operate at levels far below those which would prevail in the absence of such a law, at least until industry and transport discovered economical ways of controlling their own noxious by-products.

The consequence of recognizing such rights in one form or another, let us call them *amenity rights*, would be far-reaching. Such innovations as the invisible electronic bugging devices currently popular in the US among people eager to 'peep in' on other people's conversations could be legally prohibited in recognition of such rights.[4] The case against their use would

4. According to *Life International* (13 June 1966): 'As manufacturers leap-frog each other turning out ingenious new refinements, the components they sell have been getting smaller and more efficient. . . . So rapidly is the field developing that today's devices may be soon outmoded by systems

rest simply on the fact that the users of such devices would be unable to compensate the victims, including all the potential victims, to continue living in a state of unease or anxiety. So humble an invention as the petrol-powered lawn-mower, and other petrol-driven garden implements would come also into conflict with such rights. The din produced by any one man is invariably heard by dozens of families who, of course, may be enthusiastic gardeners also. If they are all satisfied with the current situation or could come to agreement with one another, well and good. But once amenity rights were enacted, at least no man could be forced against his will to absorb these noxious by-products of the activity of others. Of course, compensation that would satisfy the victim (always assuming he tells the truth) may exceed what the offender could pay. In the circumstances, the enthusiast would have to make do with a hand lawn-mower until the manufacturer discovered means of effectively silencing the din. The manufacturer would, of course, have every incentive to do so, for under such legislation the degree of noise-elimination would be regarded as a factor in the measurement of technical efficiency. The commercial prospects of the product would then vary with the degree of noise-elimination achieved.

Admittedly there are difficulties whenever actual compensation payments have to be made, say, to thousands of families disturbed by aircraft noise. Yet once the principle of amenity rights is recognized in law, a rough estimate of the magnitude of compensation payments necessary to maintain the welfare of the number of families affected would be entered as a matter of course into the social cost calculus. And unless these compensatory payments could also be somehow covered by the proceeds of the air service there would be no *prima facie* case for

using microcircuits so tiny that a transmitter made of them would be thinner and smaller than a postage stamp, and could be slipped undetected virtually anywhere. . . . How to safeguard individual rights in a world suddenly turned into a peep-hole and listening-post has become the toughest legal problem facing the US today.'

Whether the law could be made effective is, of course, a problem. To the extent it could not, one would have to recognize a loss of welfare arising directly from technological progress.

maintaining the air service.[5] If, on the other hand, compensatory payments could be paid (and their payment costs the company less than any technical device that would effectively eliminate the noise) some method of compensation must be devised. It is true that the courts, from time to time, have enunciated the doctrine that in the ordinary pursuit of industry a reasonable amount of inconvenience must be borne with. The recognition of amenity rights, however, does no more than impose an economic interpretation on the word 'reasonable', and therefore also on the word 'unreasonable', by transferring the cost of the inconvenience on to the shoulders of those who cause it. If by actually compensating the victims – or by paying to eliminate the disamenity by the cheapest technical method available – an existing service cannot be continued (the market being unwilling to pay the increased cost) the inconvenience that is currently being borne with is to be deemed unreasonable. And since those who cause the inconvenience are now compelled to shoulder the increased costs there should be no trouble in convincing them that the inconvenience is unreasonable and, therefore, in withdrawing the service in question.

A law recognizing this principle would have drastic effects on private enterprise which, for too long, has neglected the damage inflicted on society at large in producing its wares. For many decades now private firms have, without giving it a thought, polluted the air we breathe, poisoned lakes and rivers with their effluence, and produced gadgets that have destroyed the quiet of millions of families, gadgets that range from motorized lawnmowers and motor-cycles to transistors and private planes. What is being proposed therefore may be regarded as an alteration of the legal framework within which private firms operate in order to direct their enterprise towards ends that accord more

5. It is always open to the Government to claim that a certain air service should be maintained even though it cannot cover its social costs for reasons connected with the defence of the realm. However, it would now have to think twice about using such phrases, since it would have to vindicate its claims about the high value to the nation of this particular air service by a willingness to pay a direct subsidy to the company, from the taxpayers' money, in order to cover the costs of compensating the victims.

closely with the interests of society. More specifically, it would provide industry with the incentive necessary to undertake prolonged research into methods of removing the potential amenity-destroying features of so many of today's existing products and services.

The social advantage of enacting legislation embodying amenity rights is further reinforced by a consideration of the regressive nature of many existing external diseconomies. The rich have legal protection of their property and have less need, at present, of protection from the disamenity created by others. The richer a man is the wider is his choice of neighbourhood. If the area he happened to choose appears to be sinking in the scale of amenity he can move, if at some inconvenience, to a quieter area. He can select a suitable town house, secluded perhaps, or made soundproof throughout, and spend his leisure in the country or abroad at times of his own choosing. *Per contra*, the poorer the family the less opportunity there is for moving from their present locality. To all intents they are stuck in the area and must put up with whatever disamenity is inflicted upon it. And, generalizing from the experience of the last ten years or so, one may depend upon it that it will be the neighbourhoods of the working and lower middle classes that will suffer most from the increased construction of fly-overs and fly-unders and road-widening schemes intended to speed up the accumulating road traffic that all but poison the air. Thus the recognition of amenity rights has favourable distributive effects also. It would promote not only a rise in the standards of environment generally, it would raise them most for the lower income groups that have suffered more than any other group from unchecked 'development' and the growth of motorized traffic since the war.

7

The External Diseconomies of
Built-up Areas

THE advantages of the city are too obvious to dwell upon. Regarded as a commercial centre it may attract buyers and sellers from all over the country by offering a wide range of specialized services. In the past the city was the centre also of intellectual, artistic and scientific achievement. And today only the city, the big city or metropolis, can provide a sophisticated public large enough to form daily audiences for symphony orchestras, operas, ballets and theatres. Returning to more mundane matters, the scale of operation of such public services as water, gas, electricity, and even administration may show appreciable economies. There are, however, technological limits to the economies of size, and if such economies were the sole consideration, we might want to promote the expansion of the city until they were all fully exploited – until, that is, it was no longer possible to lower the marginal cost of any good or service by increasing the size of the city, measured either by area, population density, or wealth.

But even assuming these economies of size to be large, there are countervailing diseconomies of size. The larger the city the more time and resources have to be spent within the city on the movement of people and goods. Even telephone communication can become wasteful as the numbers in commerce and the professions increase. Any growth of building densities in city centres adds further to the difficulties of traffic that has passed the point of mutual frustration.

It might be thought that in some providential manner all this 'comes out in the wash', the right size being determined by a balance of forces in which the increasing economies are offset by increasing diseconomies. But whatever the equilibrium of forces, it is hardly one that providentially issues in a city of optimal size. There is, in fact, an asymmetry in the forces at work which tends to make the city too large. The economies of large-scale productions are apparent and there is every incentive for their exploitation by private and public companies.[1] Indeed, the more obvious external economies of a metropolitan area such as London – local availability of skilled labour and specialized personnel, accessibility to market and technical information, the provision of finance and other facilities – are so widely recognized as in fact to be overrated.[2] Even if we assumed a complete absence of countervailing forces, the scope for further exploitation of the economies of scale is likely to be negligible.[3] On the other hand, the effects of any additional population, in adding to the traffic, and ultimately in time spent commuting, in adding to the noise and grime, and the impact of this increased pressure on people's health and disposition are not taken into account by commerce and industry. Important though they are, they are difficult to measure. In the absence of pertinent legislation the incentive for expanding firms to bring them into the cost calculus is virtually non-existent.

The extent of the social damage inflicted by traffic congestion, even on itself alone, tends to be underrated by a public which

1. An 'optimal exploitation' takes place, however, only if the companies act as discriminating monopolists, or are guided by marginal-cost pricing.

2. Despite the assumption of *laissez-faire* economists that businessmen know their own interests best, there is ample evidence to show that many private firms have an *irrational* (non-commercial) preference for expanding within the metropolis rather than for setting up branches in other regions of the country. In particular, see the evidence put forward in a paper by Dr Needleman, 'What are we to do about the Regional Problem?' (*Lloyds Bank Review*, January 1965.)

3. Bear in mind also that the larger the economies of scale realized the more widespread are the effects of any accidental breakdown of public utilities, in the public transport system, the electricity supply, the telephone service or water supply. How vulnerable a large metropolis can be to a withdrawal of essential services for even a short period of time has recently been exemplified by the electricity failure (1965) and transport strike (1966) in the New York area.

habitually thinks in terms of an average figure rather than in terms of the appropriate marginal concept. A homely example illustrates the point. Three men can sit comfortably on one side of the seats of a corridor train operated by British Rail. The addition of one man will generally result in all four sitting a little too close for comfort. The additional man, in reaching a decision, need only weigh the advantage to himself of standing as against the alternative of sitting wedged between the others. He need take no account of the increased discomfort of the other three if he decides to sit down. The same principle is at work on the roads. Suppose that, over a certain period, just about a hundred cars can use a given stretch of road comfortably. Ten more cars contemplating the use of the road need reckon only the congestion to themselves. Ignoring all other social costs and assuming, for argument's sake, that the costs of congestion are the same to each motorist, the increment of cost caused by these ten is eleven times as high as the costs actually experienced by them, and on the basis of which experienced costs the ten make their decision. An unregulated traffic flow thus tends to be too large and, by one means or another, should be reduced to an 'optimal' traffic flow – one at which the marginal, or incremental, cost of congestion is equal to (or no greater than) the value placed on driving in that stream of traffic, bearing in mind the costs of all the alternative modes of travel available.

The same principle applies to the additional firm that settles in a crowded city, so adding personnel and traffic that further impede the movement of others in the city. The firm, however, need take account only of its relatively negligible share of the additional inconvenience it inflicts on everyone. Analogous remarks apply to constructing additional floor space, and to demolishing an old building in order to build a taller one with a more 'economical' use of floor space. They need take no account of the spill-over effects on the city's traffic.

Of no less topical interest is the growth of the city's population. Each person who chooses to live in the metropolis has no thought of the additional costs he necessarily imposes on others, and especially over the short period during which it is not possible to add to the existing accommodation,[4] road space or public transport facilities. In the more crowded parts of the metropolitan area it requires no more than a few thousand immigrants to reduce in remarkable degree the standard of comfort of all the previous inhabitants of the area. If the immigrants into the city happen to arrive from other parts of the country, or from other parts of the world enjoying comparable standards, the degree of discomfort suffered by the existing inhabitants, though incompatible with any optimal situation, will remain within limits. For such immigration will not continue if living conditions in such areas fall too far below the standards generally expected. If, on the other hand, immigrants come from countries with standards of living, of hygiene and comfort, well below those prevalent in the host country, the standards of the neighbourhood within which the immigrants elect to settle may have to decline drastically before the standards themselves begin to act as a disincentive to further immigration. Indeed, the immigrants may be willing to tolerate worse conditions than in the homeland since (i) those who pioneer the immigration will be prepared to endure hardship for a year or two in the hope of bettering their lot later, and (ii) some are resigned to dwell in squalid conditions for several years with the aim, initially at least, of amassing a sum of money in order either to return or to bring over their families. Moreoever, there is always a time-lag, measured perhaps in years, between the worsening of conditions in immigrant areas of the city and the general appreciation of this fact in the immigrants' homelands.

The phenomenon of external economies and diseconomies has relevance also to the physical layout of the city. A building in the city is today seldom regarded by the owners as more than a financial asset. But it may, in addition, be an asset or liability to the city. A stately building is a source of pride and pleasure to citizens while a shoddy one, of which there has been a proliferation

4. In the absence of a rise in economic rents (which would distribute the limited accommodation so as to realize an optimal situation) the additional newcomer imposes inconveniences on others in excess of his payments to the landlord.

since the war, is a source of continual annoyance and disgust. If the builder of these 'functional' modern blocks were compelled to compensate citizens for 'uglifying' their city, we might yet have hope for the future. When one considers that the architecture of the city influences the mood, the humour, even the character of its citizens; when one considers the civic pride, pleasure and sense of community that may be inspired by the architecture of a city, it is a strange reflection on our kind of civilization that we leave the initiative in designing our cities, piecemeal, largely to commercial interests, and their approval to penny-wise councillors, and we do so at a time when, more than ever before in history, pecuniary considerations are dominant.

Imagine an alternative dispensation in which some sort of ideal city is established having wide boulevards, majestic buildings, and spacious parks. The site of the city, we suppose, is owned entirely by an enlightened municipality which, as a matter of course, sets up a select committee of citizens, each of which is renowned for his taste and judgement, charged with promoting the beauty and dignity of the city.[5] If the committee become convinced of the virtues of the price mechanism to the point of willingness to sell land for development by private companies it could none the less ensure the working of 'the invisible hand', provided it sold only on condition that purchasers defrayed all relevant social costs. These would be defined to include sums of money fixed by the committee as adequate compensation to citizens who continually would have to bear unsightly or incongruent edifices plus sums to compensate for additional disamenities such as increased traffic and air pollution. Extending the market under these conditions may be expected to provide incentives to preserve and promote the beauty of the city – at least, if it did not do so, the fault could be laid squarely on the

5. The principles by which local authorities and, ultimately, the central government exercise limited control on building do not correspond with those proposed here. Local officers see themselves primarily as watchdogs of the 'public interest' guided by an *ad hoc* set of criteria. They are peculiarly vulnerable to accusations of 'holding up' progress, or discouraging growth and employment, and they can seldom resist the argument that 'development' will bring in increased revenues.

shoulders of the citizenry. Whatever the outcome one must admit the possibility of problems arising in estimating adequate compensation. But the problems arise as an inevitable result of facing the issue squarely, of attempting to bring into the calculus those social costs that are, under existing institutions, systematically ignored to the undeniable detriment of our towns and cities.[6]

In view of the rampant postwar development not only in London and other cities but also in innumerable seaside resorts and small towns of Britain, which before the war had still some remnants of local character, there is a particular urgency in recognizing these social costs. Intimate local architecture is everywhere being swamped by anonymous concrete egg-crates and the 'new' slab architecture equally suitable and equally monotonous in London, Berlin, Buenos Aires and Singapore.[7]

6. A more conservative version of this scheme, and one that does not require any institutional alteration, would seem to be to arrange for a committee of citizens to bid against the private builder in an open market. However, as we have seen, the results would not in general be the same. The maximum amount that the citizens would be willing to pay for land in order to bid it away from private use would be less than the minimum the citizens would be prepared to accept if they already owned the land. One would want to favour the method proposed in the text, however, not only for distributional reasons but also in support of the principle of vesting amenity rights in the citizens.

7. I am far from suggesting that the architect be given a free hand, though his opinions are worth hearing and would become more so were he under less pressure to seek new forms and new methods of using materials, just because they are not traditional. For a great number of people traditional materials and older styles afford far more pleasure than the modern buildings that accord with a trend towards unadorned functionalism. We still find delight in many examples of Georgian or Regency architecture. The Crescent at Regent's Park, St Paul's Cathedral, Somerset House, are justly prized not only because of their historic associations but for their inherent beauty and humanity. Much of this eighteenth- and early-nineteenth-century architecture is suggestive of the better features of those times, of spaciousness, proportion, leisure and splendour. It is with a sense of relief that the eye picks them out from the dreary uniformity of most modern city blocks. Certainly if we cannot do better than the present assortment of engineering monstrosities – from which, for monumental folly, the palm must be handed to the architects of the Elephant and Castle centre – we

had best call a halt to further building. Indeed, if we were emancipated enough to ignore strong religious feelings about 'progress', and to recognize that the new was the enemy of the excellent, a good case could be made for a programme of removing the postwar crop of eye-sores, and replacing them by an older and more intimate style of architecture.

8

External Diseconomies and
Separate Facilities

IN recognition of their being the chief legacy of the postwar period we confined ourselves, in the last two chapters, to those widespread by-products of commercial activities that are generally regarded as being socially undesirable. The proposals put forward to deal with them, however, are applicable even though different people are affected in quite different ways by particular kinds of neighbourhood effects. It may well be that some people do *not* object to the loud noises of engines operated by others; they may even revel in them. It may also be the case that some people have become so accustomed to a carbon-monoxide-polluted atmosphere as to sicken at the breath of fresh country air. And it is far from being unlikely that the postwar period has produced groups of people so habituated to uninterrupted radio noise – their own or anybody's radio – that it would unnerve them to remain long in quiet surroundings. Such people would invariably choose a transistorized beach to a quiet one. Whatever the facts in the case, and however one judges such groups, the principle of compensation, as an instrument of allocative improvement, may be extended to encompass the possibility of diverse responses. In the simplest instance, if the total compensation required by the anti-noise group were equal to or less than the total amount that the other group were ready to pay rather than do without the noise, or the noise-generating activities, there need be no interference. Provided that there were no mutually advantageous marginal reductions of noise, the existing situation is optimal. Considerations of amenity require only that those who benefit from the noise-creating activity compensate those who suffer, so maintaining the welfare of the latter group at the pre-noise level. In some cases, however, those who produce or enjoy the noise may be fewer in number, and on the average poorer, than those who deplore it, in which case the resulting optimal amount of noise is likely to be smaller.[1]

Although the principle involved in such proposals seems unassailable both on grounds of improved allocation and of social equity there are obvious practical difficulties in measuring and in implementing required compensation payments, difficulties that increase rapidly with the numbers of people that benefit or suffer in varying degrees from the activity in question. Indeed, provided we continue to treat this class of 'mixed' neighbourhood effects subject to the condition that opposite-minded groups are constrained to inhabit a common area, the principles discussed serve only to illuminate the problem: they provide little guidance for a practical solution. But there is no need at all to restrict our search for practical solutions within such a context: in considering these 'mixed' neighbourhood effects – and it is open to anyone to allege that any outstanding external diseconomy also has elements in it of external economies, or benefits – it is a distinct advantage to consider separate locations, or *separate facilities*, for the conflicting groups. The larger the proportion of a given population having different attitudes or reactions from the other members, the more practical and allocatively superior is the separate-facilities solution to a compensation-induced solution covering the whole area.

If, for example, about half the people in a large area enjoyed a transistorized beach and the other half detested it, the compensation-induced optimum would involve a reduction of transistorized noise brought about by compensation payments from

1. This optimal amount of noise may be realized (assuming each noise-maker creates the same amount of noise) beginning from the initial situation of complete quiet, and having the keenest noise-maker – judged by the highest amount he is prepared to pay to continue in the noise-creating activity – compensate the whole of the anti-noise group for tolerating the first unit of noise, the next keenest noise-maker compensating the group for the second unit of noise he will make, and so on until the nth noise-maker's maximum compensation does not suffice to meet the minimum requirements of the anti-noise group for tolerating the nth unit of noise. The outcome is optimal inasmuch as allowing a further unit of noise to be created cannot meet the criterion of an allocative improvement, that is, one that makes some people better off while making nobody worse off.

the former to the latter group. If, in reaching an optimal outcome, the latter group were exactly compensated, the transistor enthusiasts might well be somewhat better off than they would be if the law prohibited all transistors. But they would certainly be worse off than if, instead, they could revel freely in a medley of transistor noises. Providing a separate beach for transistor fans raises their welfare accordingly, while a separate beach for those wanting quiet makes them no worse off than they were under full compensation. A separate-facilities solution therefore further increases welfare – by improving the lot of transistor fans without diminishing the satisfaction of the anti-transistor group – beyond that reached by what we have called an 'optimal' solution, and may now be recognized as optimal only subject to the constraint of reaching an outcome that is common to all, which is seldom necessary.

Existing and familiar instances of separate-facilities solutions to such problems include the provision of separate smoking and non-smoking compartments in railway carriages and, in some cinemas, smoking in the balcony but not in the stalls. Pavements for pedestrians, though in a very limited way, belong to that sort of solution. And one could well multiply instances by the simple process of imagining many distinct activities being forced to share a common site, as indeed sometimes happens: for instance, a single field to be shared between soccer and rugger enthusiasts, or a single club room in which some men prefer that ladies be invited while others cannot abide so disturbing an arrangement, or in which there is a struggle over the issue of serving liquor or not. In all such cases, wherever it is practicable,[2]

2. More precisely, the value of the gain in social welfare in moving from the constrained optimal solution to the separate-facilities solution is equal to the minimum payment that had been necessary to compensate the affected members of the group for their loss of amenity (for once the latter solution is embraced such members do not lose any amenity and do not, therefore, require compensation) *plus* the maximum the erst compensators would give in order to have their separate facilities that allow them fully to indulge in the activity in question. The separate-facilities solution is, then, superior whenever this gain *added* to the saving of costs necessarily incurred in determining and maintaining the compensation-induced solution together

separate facilities increase social welfare above that reached by the constrained common-to-all optimum arrangement.

Indeed, it is of some interest in this connexion to realize that if amenity rights could be enforced at law the ordinary working of the market would tend to establish separate facilities. If, for example, the majority of people dwelling within one area preferred quiet while the majority in another area preferred motoring to the extent of being quite willing themselves to put up with the accompanying noise, motoring would be far cheaper in, and therefore, would be attracted to, the latter area. On the same principle, airlines would avoid areas where quiet was most appreciated and concentrate on routes over which compensatory payments were smallest. Even if within areas of any size opinions for and against any activity were widely dispersed the tendency to bring about separate facilities would continue to operate wherever the interests of one of the parties were highly organized, as indeed are the motoring and airline interests. Promoters of motoring would find it profitable to purchase areas of a given size (compensating the anti-motoring inhabitants either for moving or for putting up with the row) in which motoring enthusiasts could pursue their pastime unobstructed by speed limits and dwell together in roaring harmony.

Notwithstanding the operation of such a tendency in a com-

---

exceed the costs, if any, required to provide separate facilities rather than facilities in common.

In all the instances referred to in this connexion, the costs of providing separate facilities are not likely to be more than providing facilities in common for both groups. On the other hand, the gain in social welfare, and certainly that part of it identified as the minimal payment that would be necessary, under a common-to-all optimum arrangement, in order to compensate for reducing amenity, can be very high for such activities as air transport or motorized traffic, to say nothing of the costs of reaching and maintaining a constrained optimal solution. Clearly, the net social gain may be greater yet if the movement of the separate-facilities solution is not from an existing constrained optimum but, as in most cases it will be, from an existing non-optimal situation.

The use of the word practicable in the text is a loose way of indicating the condition that provision of separate facilities be low or costless, or at any rate costing less to implement than the constrained optimal solution.

munity in which amenity rights were enforceable, there is no reason why the state should not, in addition to other measures designed to promote social welfare, take the initiative itself in providing separate facilities in order that the wants of those for whom quiet, clean air, and pleasant environment were highly valued could be met without prejudice to those who 'couldn't care less'. Even if it transpired, which I very much doubt, that people who value such things are a small minority, the principle of amenity rights still warrants the creation of separate facilities for their enjoyment.[3] Any government at all concerned with the welfare of individuals, or any government that is guided by economists prone to stress the goal of increasing the range of choices open to the individual, could not excuse itself from making a start by setting aside large residential areas through which no motorized traffic is permitted to pass and over which no aircraft is permitted to fly, or from prohibiting motor-boats on the lakes in certain districts, and traffic in general from such lake districts. Municipalities should be able to make a start by providing stretches of beach free from transistor noise (while, of course, freely allowing it along other parts of the beach), by keeping motor traffic away from certain shopping areas, from narrow roads, from cathedral precincts, and other places of beauty or historic interest that can be enjoyed only in a quiet traffic-free setting.

And surely such proposals seem reasonable enough in themselves without labouring their economic rationale. After all, there is already too much of a muchness; every road crawling with

3. One of the oft-alleged virtues of the price system, in comparison with the system of decisions based on majority voting, is that a properly functioning price system is responsive to minority tastes. Even in the context in which this generalization is commonly understood, its truth depends largely upon the organization of the market and the existing technology. Nevertheless, once a stage is reached in economic development beyond which the generation of external diseconomies competes with the generation of the national product, the wants of minorities – and even those of majorities – are increasingly ignored by the private enterprise price system. Only political power is then able to redress this social evil either through government intervention, direct and indirect, and/or through legislation establishing rights of amenity.

automobiles, the air of every town and village fouled with their gas, to be relished by all who have stomach enough for these things. No enthusiastic 'pace-maker' need feel himself deprived if some areas in Britain are set aside for the quiet-loving minority – if it is a minority. Nor should all such areas display the same features; there is room enough for a wide range of social experiment in living together. One need have no objection whatsoever to developing areas specifically for the enthusiastic motor-cyclists, for the 'young in heart' and for the would-be young, over which they could ride around for hours without unavoidably annoying those whose tastes run to other things. At the other extreme, decent residential areas could be set aside for those backward-looking people who would be glad to abolish the use of all engines outside the home and for eccentrics who would prefer to dwell in areas admitting only horses and horse-drawn vehicles as means of transport. If they are prepared to pay for it – and there is no reason why any such arrangement should cost more to operate, rather than less, compared with existing modern arrangements – there is no advantage to the rest of the country in depriving them of their wants.[4] In between, there should be a wide variety, some areas having no more than large pedestrian precincts, or traffic-free shopping islands, to distinguish them, others permitting only public transport or electrically-powered transport on their roads, others yet prohibiting all types of motorized vehicles, or prohibiting them between certain hours, and many of them refusing airline compensation in order to remain free from aerial disturbance.[5]

4. All such relatively 'primitive' areas would presumably be connected with the rest of the country by rail, though of course the wishes of the inhabitants would be taken into consideration.

5. There should be no great difficulty in determining the right size of and number of any particular type of separate facility. Larger numbers of people per square yard, or square mile, congregating in type A facility compared with type B might be taken as an index of the increased popularity of type A compared with B, and steps taken to increase the size and/or number of them until some equilibrium were established. In comparing different types of residential areas, however, there should be no objection to guidance by market forces. Once the range of alternative areas has been sufficiently

With almost all the convenient and desirable areas close to the metropolis, and with many other desirable towns and villages already shaped for a motorized society, heavy capital costs may have to be incurred in 'reconverting' suitable places to amenity areas. In conformity with the principles laid down in this and previous chapters, however, if the value to potential inhabitants of any such amenity area – estimated as the minimum sum required to compensate them in forgoing their legal rights to amenity – exceeds the capital costs of converting the area, social welfare and equity is advanced in creating such an area.

Business economists have ever been glib in equating economic growth with an expansion of the range of choices facing the individual; they have failed to observe that as the carpet of 'increased choice' is being unrolled before us by the foot, it is simultaneously being rolled up behind us by the yard. We are compelled willy-nilly to move into the future that commerce and technology fashions for us without appeal and without redress. In all that contributes in trivial ways to his ultimate satisfaction, the things at which modern business excels, new models of cars and transistors, prepared foodstuffs and plastic *objets d'art*, electric toothbrushes and an increasing range of push-button gadgets, man has ample choice. In all that destroys his enjoyment of life, he has none. The environment about him can grow ugly, his ears assailed with impunity, and smoke and foul gases exhaled over his person. He may be in circumstances that he will never enjoy a night's rest at home without planes shrieking overhead. Whether he is indifferent to such circumstances, whether he bears them stoically, or whether he writhes in impotent fury, there is under the present dispensation practically nothing he can do about them.

To conclude, extension of choice in respect of environment is the one really significant contribution to social welfare that is immediately feasible. As suggested, however, it is not likely to be

increased, the relative size and number of, say, type C and type D areas may be determined by the demand for them. All that is required is imagination in the design of such areas and initiative in their provision.

brought about by market forces working within the given legal framework. Legal recognition of amenity rights, on the other hand, would touch off government, and private, initiative in creating a wide diversity of residential environment offering to all men those vital choices that have too long been denied them.

The Dereliction of the City (i)

I

LET us pause for a while at this juncture to contemplate modern society's greatest nightmare, motorized traffic. The city is a centre point of civilization, as a place of human concourse and life and gaiety, is becoming a thing of the past. Hoarse beneath the fumes emitted by an endless swarm of crawling vehicles, today's city bears close resemblance to some gigantic and clamorous arsenal. None of the present piecemeal attacks on the sorest affliction of twentieth-century society have led to any noticeable improvement. The transport economist's solution does not take one very far. As indicated above, one can estimate marginal congestion costs and infer some 'optimal' traffic flow which, as suggested in Appendix C, need not be very different from the existing flow – but only by ignoring, often explicitly, the so-called intangibles that can be by far the more important part of the external diseconomies inflicted by traffic on the city. The same blind eye is in evidence when estimating 'optimal' parking charges or the rate of return on road-building, and when wielding the now fashionable technique of cost-benefit analysis. Sometimes, as a gesture of technical bravado, economists may add to the social cost of motorized traffic an estimate of the costs to the community of the number of fatal accidents by the felicitous device of reckoning the cost of a man killed as the loss of his potential future pecuniary contribution to the national product. At any rate, it is a device that has the virtue of keeping the cost low to the motoring community as the trend continues towards an increasing proportion of aged people in the total kill. Many of the aged, of course, contribute practically nothing to the national product and, on this principle therefore, their loss to the nation is negligible.[1]

1. An unqualified rejection of this principle has been made in an early

The piecemeal methods of engineers in the face of traffic problems differ from those of the economist only in being cruder. They turn on the location of 'growing points' in the traffic, and on a variety of formulae, based on traffic growth relative to road capacity, that yield critical ratios purporting to justify increased investment. These formulae are supplemented by *ad hoc* decisions on building bridges, circuses, by-passes, diversions, fly-overs and fly-unders, whenever something 'has to be done'. If the engineers could save us by such methods, or by even more grandiose ones, we should by now have had ample evidence of their success from the United States where, in many cities, municipalities' engineers have been bending over backwards for years in the endeavour to accommodate the motorist. Yet no relief is in sight. Far from it, cities like New York, Detroit, Los Angeles, lie prostrate beneath traffic that crawls about like armies of locusts devouring the very heart and soul of the city. One might have thought we could, as a nation, save ourselves some bitter experiences by tearing a page from the American diary. Apparently, however, we are determined to subject ourselves to the same experience by using the same piecemeal approach, albeit more cautiously, in response to the growing traffic until we reach the same situation of near chaos. For the overall response of governments since the war has been to do little more than to make stern noises about efficiency while

---

paper by Professor Eli Devons, 'The Language of Economic Statistics', reprinted in *Essays in Economics* (1961).

A more meaningful economic measure of the cost of accidents would be the compensation necessary to induce each individual in the community to accept the risks associated with motoring *under present conditions*. Some, of course, would be glad to stick their necks out for nothing. At the other extreme would be those who could hardly be bribed by any price if there were any choice in the matter. At this other extreme we might have to answer the question: how much should the motor-enthusiast have to pay the potential corpse for depriving him of life and liberty? There is more than one way of reckoning the social costs of a pastime that has the incidental effect of killing off one's fellows. And reckoning it the hard way – at unimaginably large sums necessary to satisfy those who want to be no part of the motorized society – seems right to me, even if it would entail the abolition of private motoring in any collective choice.

allowing, nay encouraging, the use of the nation's limited resources to install more plant to produce more cars, lorries, and scooters, that show a profit to their makers, and a gain to their users, by steadfastly ignoring the mounting costs of traffic control, of mutual frustration, and of the barely tolerable pressure of noise, stench, dirt and exasperation, to say nothing of the increasing figures for death and mutilation. For the popular journalist, impatient of tomorrow's cornucopia of gadgets, the accumulation of disamenities and the vexations of modern living may be no more than the 'inevitable costs of progress'. But properly classified by the economist they constitute an immense tangle of external diseconomies that, partly by their nature but more by historical accident, have escaped the costing mechanism.

So far only one radical proposal appears to have been put forward by the engineers to meet the road problem, that in the famous report by Professor Colin Buchanan, who was asked in 1962 by Mr Marples, the then Minister of Transport, to 'study the long-term development of roads and traffic in urban areas and their influence on urban environment'. Buchanan became convinced of one thing: that present developments could not be allowed to continue. Unless something was done soon, he warned the public, the usefulness of vehicles in towns would decline rapidly, and pleasantness and safety would 'deteriorate catastrophically'. He rejected the Government's then existing policy of small-scale road improvements designed to keep the traffic moving at all costs as being self-defeating. Such 'improvements' would, he prophesied, be overtaken by the increase in traffic as soon as they were finished.[2] Yet, notwithstanding his graphic descriptions of the damage and disamenity wrought on our lives by the private automobile, he based his recommendations on premises similar to those furnished in the Report's introduction

2. A 'Parkinson's Law' for traffic: that private motoring expands so as to fill the road space made available, is readily explained by the existing motoring potential and its growth relative to the physical constraints. At the time of writing, for instance, of the total number of private car-owners in the London area only an estimated 7 per cent use them for commuting into central London.

by Sir Geoffrey Crowther: that the motor-car was 'a potentially highly beneficial invention' and its future was assured. There were 10½ million vehicles in 1962. By 1970 we could expect this number to increase to 18 million. By 1980 there should be some 27 million vehicles on our roads, growing to about 40 million by the end of the century. Apparently it would be futile to fight against this trend, as it appeared that the population was as intent on owning cars as were the manufacturers in providing them.

Starting from such 'modernistic' propositions it is not surprising that Buchanan goes on to argue that if the present-day town is unsuitable for the motor-car then it must be rebuilt so that we can have the traffic we want along with the amenity we also seek. Having established a need for his expertise he proceeds to consider the various principles of road construction such as the corridor system which would set up 'environmental areas' within an interlacing network of highways. In particular he lays stress on the need for 'traffic architecture' which involves an integration of buildings and roads at different levels.

But before succumbing to the futuristic visions of benevolent technocrats, the economist should pause to consider the full social costs of their attempted implementation in this already overpacked island of ours, costs that are better appreciated by comparing Buchanan's proposals not with the existing chaos – which would, admittedly, render it attractive – but rather with other radical alternatives. For even if the social costs of the existing situation, of the Buchanan Plan and of the alternatives to it are not easily measurable, the public's range of choice is broadened by revealing to it technologically feasible opportunities hitherto unconsidered. In the particular case of transport, with its pervasive repercussions on our ways of living, such alternatives must necessarily include schemes of resource-allocation other than those presented to us either by the existing market mechanisms, modified by a patchwork of government regulations, or by the humane aspirations of engineers.

II

The social significance of both the market and the engineering criteria involved, as well as that of the alternative solution proposed here, may be better understood if, for a while, we skirt direct controversy and approach these issues by a sort of parable. Thus, without straining his credulity perhaps, the reader may be able to picture to himself a region of some continent, say, on the other side of the Atlantic in which the traditional right to carry firearms is never questioned. Indeed, on the initiative of the manufacturers, who spend colossal sums in advertising their new wares, more than one pistol is to be seen in a man's belt. The young men in particular are anxious to be seen with the latest de luxe 'extra hard-hitting' model. Obviously the manufacture of holsters and other accessories flourishes as also does the manufacture of bullet-proof vests, leggings and helmets. These are not the only growth industries, however, for notwithstanding the purchase of bullet-proof items, the members of the undertakers' association do a flourishing trade. The windows of all but the poorer houses are fitted with shatter-proof glass, while the bullet-proofing of rooms and offices in the more dangerous districts is a matter of ordinary precautions. No family is foolish enough to neglect the training of their sons, and even their daughters, in the art of the quick draw. In any case, a number of hours each week is devoted to target practice and dodgery in all the best schools. Life insurance is, of course, big business despite the exorbitant premiums, and expenditure on medical attention continues to soar. For in addition to such normal ailments as bullets embedded in various parts of the anatomy, there is widespread suffering from a variety of chafed skin diseases, the result of wearing the unavoidably heavy bullet-proof apparel. Moreover, owing to nervous diseases and anxiety, about every other adult is addicted either to strong liquor or to tranquillizing drugs. Taxes are burdensome for obvious reasons: a swollen police force employed mainly in trying to keep down the number of victims of the perennial feuds, extensive prisons and prison hospitals, to say nothing of the public funds devoted to guarding offices, banks, schools, and to the construction of special vans for transporting the children to and from schools.

In such an environment the most peace-loving man would be foolish to venture abroad unarmed. And since it is observed by the *laissez-faire* economist that men freely choose to buy guns, it would be regarded as an infringement of liberty to attempt to curb their manufacture. Moreover, since the market is working smoothly, the supply of firearms being such that no one need wait if he is able to pay the market price, no government intervention to match industrial supplies to rising demand is called for. Provided there is enough competition in the production of firearms so that over the long period prices just cover costs (and tend also to equal marginal costs of production) the allocation economist is well satisfied. Looking at the promising signs of growth in the chief industries, firearms and accessories, the business economist pronounces the economy 'sound'. If, however, for any reason the Government begins to have misgivings about some of the more blatant social repercussions, it consults with the pistol economist, a highly paid and highly regarded expert. The pistol economist constructs models and, with the help of high-powered statisticians, amasses pistological data of all kinds, from which he calculates the optimal set of taxes on the sale of pistols and ammunition in recognition of those external diseconomies, such as occasional corpse-congestion on the better streets, whose monetary costs can, he believes, be estimated.

Notwithstanding all his scientific advice, matters eventually come to a head, and amid much government fanfare a committee of inquiry is set up under the chairmanship of a highly competent engineer, Mr B. If there ever was a realist, Mr B. is one, and he soon satisfies himself that the economy is heavily dependent upon pistol production, and all the auxiliary industries and services connected therewith. Besides, the evidence is incontrovertible: the demand for guns continues to grow year by year. It must, therefore, be accepted as a datum. Undaunted, Mr B. faces 'the challenge' by proposing a radical remodelling of the chief towns and cities, at an unmentionable cost, in the endeavour to create an environment in which people can have both their guns and a peaceful life as well. The chief features of his plan are based on what he aptly calls 'pistol architecture', and includes provision for no-shooting precincts fenced high with steel, the construction of circular and wavy road design to increase the difficulties of gun-duelling, the erection of high shatter-proof glass screens running down the centres of roads to prevent effective cross-firing, and the setting up of heavily protected television cameras at all strategic positions in the towns in order to relay information twenty four hours a day to a vast new centralized police force equipped with fleets of helicopters. Every progressive journalist pays tribute to the foresight and realism of the B-plan and makes much of the virtues of 'pistol architecture', the architecture of the future. Alas, the government begins to realize that any attempt to raise the taxes necessary to implement the B-Plan would start a revolution. So the plan is quietly shelved, new committees of inquiry are formed, masses of agenda are produced, and things continue much as before.

III

We need not continue save to press home a few parallels. Chiefly under the impetus of the automobile, the suburbs are pushing their way farther out into the countryside in a vain endeavour by commuters to 'get away from it all'. An environment is thus created in which, while it is increasingly exhausting to travel, it becomes increasingly indispensable for many to have a private car. The very existence of the private motor-car encourages the geographical dispersion of housing, of shops, of entertainment, and of a variety of consumer services, which spread in its turn increases the indispensability of the private automobile. From an aggregative approach, the private automobile sometimes appears indispensable for another reason; namely, that a large part of our economy, a swiftly growing part too, is geared to automobile production. Like the Americans, we in this country are cultivating a dependence, perhaps as much psychological as economic, on the car industry and all its ramifications. Vested interests have grown and become formidable. They bar the road to consideration of all radical innovations that threaten their establishment.[3]

The alternative to the Buchanan Plan emerging from the story is, quite plainly, not to seek to develop technological means of *accommodating* the mounting traffic but, quite the contrary, to seek to *contain* it. Indeed, the one radical alternative we should take a long look at, before contemplating the range of compromise solutions that are feasible, is that of a plan for the gradual abolition of all privately owned automobiles.

For a fraction of the money the nation is currently spending on the maintenance of private cars and on the Government services necessary to keep the traffic moving – to say nothing of the cost of all the external diseconomies already described – we could simultaneously achieve three desirable objectives: (1) provide a comfortable, frequent and highly efficient public transport service, bus, train, or tube, in all the major population areas (and, in the interest of quiet and clean air, preferably electrically-powered transport),[4] (2) through government control of public transport, restrain and gradually reverse the spread of population that has followed in the wake of postwar speculative building and is in the process of transforming the south-east into an uninterrupted suburban region, and (3) restore quiet and dignity to our cities, and enable people to wander unobstructed by traffic and enjoy once more the charm of historic towns and villages.[5]

Further radical changes would, of course, have to be made in the organization of freight delivery if we are successfully to

3. According to the *Economist* (11 June 1966): 'Traffic congestion is Rome's most obvious problem. The old city, with its narrow streets, simply will not take the growing flood of private cars. . . . There are brilliant paper plans to stop the chaos but the political courage to carry them out is lacking. A new ring-road is being built, but so far every attempt to discipline traffic in the centre has collapsed at the first contact with vested interests.'

4. The provisional continuation of a taxi service in the metropolis should be conceded (on condition the taxis were fitted with anti-fume devices) in order to prevent abuses arising from any exemption in favour of privileged groups such as doctors or ministers of the crown.

5. When one considers the reliance on the modern automobile by organized crime, especially by the robbery-and-violence gangs, one is tempted to claim for the scheme an inevitable and immense reduction of city crime.

avoid massive investment in refashioning our cities to cater for the growing commercial traffic. The movement of such freight should be minimized (*a*) by substituting as far as possible existing railways in the built-up areas during off-peak hours, (*b*) similarly, by adapting and extending London's Underground to carry freight, initially during the night, and (*c*) removing freight deliveries from a multitude of small and large firms and placing them instead under a single authority in order, like the post office, to avail ourselves of the economies of coordination. Finally, in order to maintain the environment of the city, the possibilities of organizing shop deliveries at times when people are off the streets, say between three and seven in the mornings, deserves careful study.[6]

At any rate – if we are to have a single solution for the country at large – here is one alternative solution towards which we might advance, a radical one to be sure, but technically practicable, and one providing a relatively inexpensive way, in terms of money and lives,[7] of establishing a more civilized pattern of living.

6. An outright prohibition against freight deliveries during the day need not be introduced initially in such an experiment. For instance, one could permit vehicles free access during the night hours while imposing a levy on those wishing to use the streets outside these hours. Moreover only electrically-powered vehicles might be allowed with speed limits not exceeding, say, 15 miles per hour.

One incidental advantage to the British consumer of such a scheme would be to encourage shops to hold larger inventories than they do at present. (Shops would, in any case, choose to hold larger inventories if the true costs of currently transporting their goods had to be borne by them.)

7. The public should be made aware that in choosing to continue with the present system, in choosing the private car rather than public transport, it also implicitly chooses to sacrifice the lives of many thousands of citizens and to cripple for life a great many more. Currently we write off the lives of over seven thousand men, women and children each year and about ten times that number seriously injured. In the United States, with far greater experience of motoring than we, and with better roads built to carry more traffic at higher speeds, the community has been brought up to accept an annual sacrifice of lives now running at forty-six thousand a year. The sacrifice of a life or two by primitive communities in the belief that it ensured a good harvest seems humane in comparison with the implicit decision

It is not a solution that will be presented to us by the market, however, and understandably, not one that will be proposed to us by the technocrats, yet it is one that is worthy of consideration by a nation that prides itself on its social awareness and political maturity. In the meantime, local plans to prohibit motor-cars, during certain hours at least, from designated special areas in resorts, historic towns, and city centres – in London, certainly the area about Soho, including Piccadilly Circus and Leicester Square, so that, as in times gone by, people may stroll freely through the city streets enjoying once more the hubbub and gaiety of human voices, and recapturing perhaps a lost sense of community and citizenship – will make some modest contribution towards making the physical environment more enjoyable.

The only alternatives to this radical solution that are both feasible and inexpensive are those based on the principle of 'separate facilities', already discussed; in other words the provision of large viable areas for those citizens who want, with varying degrees of intensity, to opt out of the environment of mounting disamenity and disaster created by the private automobile and air travel.

But within the city, at least, there can be no socially acceptable solution to the traffic problem that aims to accommodate the private automobile. Continuation of the present policy of attempting to do so by piecemeal alterations leads ultimately to the crucifixion of the city by its traffic – an epithet that just about describes what has happened in Los Angeles.

---

to kill some tens of thousands yearly that the pleasures of private motoring be upheld.

The Government, aware of the rising figures, salves its conscience by endlessly exhorting us to be more careful while, at the same time, permitting motor-car manufacturers and oil companies to goad the public, especially the impressionable young, to ever faster speeds. And while the oil companies are urging motorists to 'put tigers in their tanks' the Government connives by imposing unbelievably lenient accident laws. At the time of writing a man who was driving at 60 miles per hour was fined £1,500 for simultaneously killing a woman and her daughter. This works out at £750 per head, a sum that compares favourably with the cost of licence to kill an elephant in Africa. Yet the newspapers reported that it was the highest fine that had ever been imposed for this offence.

The Dereliction of the City (ii)

I

MEN have become the victims of their faith in progress. Owing to the institutional framework lagging in crucial respects behind economic developments, men are under the illusion that they have freely chosen the private automobile as the conveyance of the future. Like Buchanan, they have unthinkingly come to accept it as an inescapable fact of modern living. Yet what is really crying out for modernization is not technology but the institutional framework of the economy. Until we succeed in modernizing this institutional framework we shall continue to encounter difficulties in bringing into the terms of choice that people should face a variety of social costs that escape all conventional accounting. Under an institutional framework which, among other effects, had that of saddling the motorists with defraying to the full all social costs, including compensatory payments for reducing the amenity of others, the traffic problem would disappear of itself.

One might have hoped that considerations such as these would have been brought to the attention of the public by the so-called transport economist to which, in despair, the Government is now turning for guidance – it being one of the persistent illusions of twentieth-century governments that no social problem can long withstand the combined brain power and know-how of a large enough body of scientists, engineers, statisticians and economists. However, it is not just the alleged conflict of purposes in the Ministry of Transport, as between planners, engineers, administrators and economists, that is holding matters up. One may now safely assume that the influence of the transport economist is in the ascendant – a fact which would be heartening if all roads were somehow removed from their environment and situated instead somewhere in the moon or in the more desolate parts of the earth. But since the traffic problem is to be found largely within the cities, towns and suburbs, and the problem is, therefore, one of social welfare in general, the transport economist, as it happens, is not the man to consult. For the transport economist addresses himself in the main to the mutual frustration experienced by the increasing traffic; that is, only to those external diseconomies that additional traffic impose on existing traffic, and not with costs imposed by traffic as a whole on the rest of society. If he cannot, or will not, measure the latter costs, his calculations of the rates of return on existing roads, of the benefit-cost ratios of traffic investment, and of the 'optimal traffic flows' within towns and cities remain without allocative significance.

To be plain, the expertise that the transport economist can bring to bear on traffic problems in town and city is largely bogus. I do not allege that he is consciously perpetrating a fraud. Like all too many men in the social sciences he is impatient to display his scientific credentials, anxious to be seen measuring, that is, even where it entails, as it so manifestly does in this case, measuring much the smaller part of the problem for lack of a method to capture the larger. Since I wish these allegations to be taken seriously I shall spell them out carefully to avoid any misunderstanding.

First, then, it is alleged that the transport economist by and large confines his models to measuring the costs on traffic generated by traffic, mutual congestion costs, and ignores or relegates to parenthetical remarks the widespread accumulation of effects on the environment: not only the dirt and dust, the noise and smell, and the distraction and tenseness caused by the uninterrupted pressure of traffic always about us but also the growing dehumanization of the physical environment in response to mounting traffic. Roads and buildings are constructed with the needs of motorized traffic in mind, not of pedestrians. He ignores also the role of the motor-car as the chief instrument, in the postwar period, for spreading subtopia over the countryside of Britain. These social costs, it may be alleged, arise from repercussions that are so widespread and interconnected as to defy, at present, any acceptable method of valuation. But to ignore them in all decisions bearing on road traffic is irresponsible. At a guess, I should put the measurable congestion costs of the transport economist at not more than one twentieth of the total of social costs generated by motorized traffic, the remaining nineteen twentieths being accounted for by the so-called intangibles. Whether or not others go along with these impressionistic figures, no one, surely, will deny the evidence of his senses which tells him that the private automobile is the most potent influence since the war in shaping the environment around us.

Second, the device employed for measuring benefits to the motoring population is perverse. No matter what their degree of sophistication very few of the commonly used transport models fail to draw on the notion of 'consumers' surplus' – a measure that is approximately represented by the area under the price-demand curve – as an indicator of benefits. Whether they are concerned with (a) benefit-cost ratios, (b) the internal rate of return on a new road or bridge, or (c) the determination of the so-called 'optimal traffic flow' (a procedure that takes account of the congestion costs imposed by each additional vehicle on the traffic as a whole), this measure of consumers' surplus is, generally, an essential part of the calculation.

Yet, as I have shown elsewhere,[1] the consumers' surplus measure of benefit can be used as an approximation only under peculiarly restrictive conditions, particular attention being paid to the constancy of the prices of the alternative opportunities available. By neglecting this crucial condition the resulting measure of consumers' surplus is not merely unreliable. In the circumstances in which it is used by transport economists it is possible, even likely, that the resulting measure of benefit is *inversely* related to the actual benefit: thus, as the welfare of the motoring population declines the consumers' surplus measure may well register increasing benefit – a contingency that seems to have escaped the attention of some transport economists. For this reason I have discussed it more formally in Appendix C.

1. 'A Survey of Welfare Economics 1939–1959', *Economic Journal*, June 1960.

II

Before moving on, let us illustrate the nature of two interrelated kinds of decision necessary to uncover a range of separate-facilities opportunities that are alternative to the overall solution proposed in the preceding part of this digression.

(A) First, there are decisions to be taken about the particular features of traffic control within any area, which may involve one or more of the following: at one extreme (i) all motorized transport of any description to be excluded; (ii) only public transport permitted, supplemented, or not, by a taxi service; (iii) commercial vehicles within the precincts of the city, town, or suburb not permitted during the day; (iv) commercial vehicles permitted if electrically powered, with or without extra charge; (v) whatever traffic permitted, all of it subject to drastic speed limits; (vi) permitted traffic confined to certain roads; (vii) Post Office to take over and coordinate all freight deliveries.

(B) Second, there have to be decisions about the size of the areas themselves over which any of the above features, or combination of such features, is to be established. (i) The minimum non-motoring area could, of course, be no smaller than a conventional pedestrian precinct found within certain towns or suburbs; (ii) in addition, ancient, winding, or narrow streets, or secluded squares could be set aside purely for the convenience of pedestrians; (iii) central parts of some cities and towns, and the more picturesque and historic parts, could be cleared of all motorized traffic; (iv) some town and city centres entire could be freed of all private and commercial traffic; (v) some cities, towns and suburbs may be freed wholly of all private motoring; (vi) select regions, districts, and whole counties might be made available for all those wishing to escape the proximity and consequences of private motoring and air travel.

A number of difficult decisions must inevitably crop up in arranging the transition from the present unrelieved traffic nightmare to any one of a variety of solutions. Since I am pointing out the main features of a solution and not presenting a blueprint to the Government I shall not discuss them here – though it need never be doubted that those who feel their interests threatened will make the most of them to prevent a change of direction from the present policy of drift into traffic chaos. However, the precondition of any social advance is that people become convinced of the existence of many practical alternatives to the present policy, alternatives offering a wide range of choice, hitherto denied them in that most vital of influences affecting their welfare, the physical environment itself in which they dwell and work.

9

External Diseconomies and
Social Conflict

I

THE rapid growth of unresolved external diseconomies associated with post-war affluence manifests itself not only as continued distortion in the use of our national resources but also, in some cases, as a sharpening of conflict between opposed interests. One that is coming to a head in the United States just now is the conflict between those enterprises that for years have been pouring their waste products into the once-fresh waters of lakes and rivers and the public at large, a fact of life that is belatedly being discovered by journalists and by citizens who are being deprived of the use of such waters for drinking, fishing or bathing. At the time of writing (August 1965) the city of New York, apprehensive of an impending water shortage, can no longer tap the apparently readiest source of supply, the Hudson River, which is now poisonous from years of cumulative pollution. Of course, if it were otherwise, if fresh water were everywhere abundant – which has been the prevailing conviction in this country and in the United States and one which might have been justified before the war – there would be no good reason why it should not be used wastefully and fouled by industry. In view of the extent and growth of water pollution, it is safer and simpler to enact general laws against fouling fresh water, spoiling beaches with oil, sewage, etc. (unless, in particular cases, it is demonstrably in the public interest not to do so) rather than seek to regulate waste-disposal by complicated formulae intended to realize an ideal correction. The West is sufficiently rich to make amends for past follies by erring on the generous side in preserving for posterity limited natural resources that, in the absence of prohibition or regulation, would continue to be spoiled and to be squandered.

A more menacing source of conflict at this stage in world

history, though people appear reluctant to recognize the fact, is that arising from continued population expansion and, more recently, mass migration. In very poor countries, such as India, the 'classical' economic situation is still to be found: a growing population pressing on limited natural resources, and a tendency, therefore, for the incomes of property-owners to rise while, in general, living standards settle near bare subsistence. Although this Malthusian situation is a thing of the past within Western Europe, there still remains the potent threat of further movements of indigenous population, in particular of motorized population, into urban areas. Such movements continue to press on limited space so as to make the physical environment in which we live increasingly disagreeable.

To financial columnists and growthmen, one of the factors insistently stressed as being conducive to rapid economic expansion is the growth of population whether contributed by immigrant or indigenous sources. Indeed, on this view it is not so much *per capita* 'real' growth that alone is desirable, but total real growth. A growth-obsessed government setting itself the task of increasing aggregate real income by, say, 25 per cent over some short period may be tempted to achieve its goal simply by importing labour, even if the imported labour happened to be less efficient than domestic labour. Those who have gone overboard in their passion for growth, as have many influential persons in the Common Market countries, do not hesitate at the idea of augmenting population from outside countries. And certainly one need anticipate no opposition from the business world, whose interests are served by an expanding market however brought about, nor from landlords, who contemplate with equanimity the rise in rents caused by the competition of increasing population for a fixed supply of land.[1]

1. Rising economic rent in response to increasing population is one way of coping with, or correcting, the incidence of an external diseconomy caused by increasing numbers of people seeking to settle within a given area. Though a well-functioning market promotes optimal adjustment in respect of this particular form of external diseconomy, regressive distributional effects can be a source of conflict.

Moreoever, the achievement of optimality is no assurance against a

To put the matter bluntly, there are no longer vast inhabitable areas to be peopled in Western Europe. And though freedom to move is an ancient and cherished freedom, the scale of potential immigration into Europe from poor countries is today fraught with social and economic consequences that are far from being beneficial to the indigenous populations. Inasmuch as net immigration acts to reduce the amount of land *per capita* available, real rents rise; inasmuch as immigrants from the poor countries are for the main part unskilled and without capital assets there is an initial reduction in the capital-income ratio of the host country. In addition, since net immigration of labour acts to raise the returns to land and capital, the distributional effects tend to be regressive, the extent of these effects depending, *inter alia*, on the scale of immigration, on the rate of capital accumulation, on the innovating processes, and on the technical difficulty of substituting capital in industry.

Moreover, large-scale immigration is not only likely to be socially unsettling, in an economy as close to full employment as the United Kingdom has been since the war it is almost sure to have a net inflationary impact on the economy.[2] A large-scale inflow of relatively unskilled labour therefore acts as a distributionally regressive force (inasmuch as profits and, to a lesser extent, wages increase at the expense of fixed income groups including pensioners). In addition, an increase of population from abroad, like an increase in the indigenous population, raises the demand for imports (even in the complete absence of upward pressure on domestic prices) without inducing a corres-

---

worsening situation. An economy may be moving from one optimal position to another, each optimal position corresponding to a deteriorating situation. For example, if, because of immigrant population flows, land per inhabitant declines there exists, notwithstanding a continued optimal use of land, a divergence of material interests between the existing number of inhabitants and potential immigrants. The material interests in wealthy, but small, countries is however, very much less important than their interest in preserving amenity.

2. For some estimates of excess primary aggregate demand generated by immigration, see 'Immigration: Some Economic Effects' by Mishan and Needleman in *Lloyds Bank Review*, July 1966.

ponding increase of exports thereby worsening the balance-of-payments position – or worsening the terms of trade in the longer run.[3] Nonetheless, I am inclined to rate very much higher than these untoward economic effects the impact of large-scale immigration on the existing diseconomies of an already too-large-for-comfort population and the already intractable traffic problem. These diseconomies will necessarily be aggravated and frequently localized by immigration into this rather tight little island.[4]

It may be observed in passing that this conflict between the existing inhabitants of a region and would-be immigrants is also to be found within the frontiers of a single country. For instance, according to Professor Raymond Dasmann,[5] the beauty and natural resources of California are being destroyed by the rapid influx of Americans from other States. 'Everywhere', writes Dasmann, 'crowding destroys the values that the people who

3. It is sometimes argued in the popular press that this country benefits from immigrants' willingness to enter unpopular occupations where services are maintained without raising costs to the public. This is, however, a one-sided analysis. When account is taken of the domestic opportunities for improved allocation in the absence of immigration the argument no longer holds. This topic among others has been discussed by Dr Needleman and myself in a paper on the longer term economic consequences of large-scale immigration, *Lloyds Bank Review.* January 1968.

4. It is a sad reflection on our times that scientists interested in the 'population explosion' are concerned for the most part with the purely technical problem of feeding the swelling populations. Schemes range from more high-powered animal farms to processing grass, and from exploiting the seas to making plastic meat substitutes.

That already man has broken all ecological bounds and that, unless one can somehow reverse the trends, the world's population will have doubled by the end of the century; that thereafter we shall be as thick as locusts over many parts of the inhabitable earth – all this is as nothing to the vision of growthmen who continue to exorcize any future spectre with the word challenge.

5. Raymond F. Dasmann, *The Destruction of California* (Macmillan, 1965). In an endeavour to check the gradually declining quality of life in California, Dasmann suggests a stop to the building of more freeways, power stations, and residential accommodation in order to discourage potential immigrants. Needless to relate, California's businessmen and government officials brush Dasmann's solution aside.

crowd in come to seek.' Lake Tahoe, the largest and perhaps the most beautiful mountain lake in the United States, became the fashionable place to go to after the Second World War. 'Nevada gamblers began to build skyscraper hotels. ... Seepage and effluent from sewage treatment plants began to pour ... into the once clear water.' Now, like other lakes in the United States, Tahoe is on its way to becoming an algae-fouled cesspool.

II

From the destruction wrought by large population movements to that wrought by mass tourism is a short step and one that opens up a vista of the immeasuable destructive potential of indiscriminate economic growth. In the last decade alone there has been something of a holocaust of the scarcest of our earthly resources, natural beauty. In this instance the conflict of interest is between, on the one hand, the tourists, tourist agencies, traffic industries and ancillary services, to say nothing of governments anxious to augment their reserves of foreign currencies, and all those who care about preserving natural beauty on the other.

There is obviously also a conflict of interest between present and future generations. It is true that a sizeable fraction of mankind forms part of a regular tourist invasion, but this is the result of pricing travel well below the social costs incurred. For the cost to the marginal tourist takes no account of the additional congestion costs he imposes on all others (tourists and inhabitants or of the additional loss of quiet and fresh air, or of the scenic destruction suffered by all in consequence of additional building required). Moreover, it is clear to the most reverent nature-lover that any personal sacrifice he makes will have no practical effect in reducing mass tourism, any more than his refusal to drive an automobile would reverse the trend towards increasing city congestion. If anything, there is an incentive for him to travel the sooner, and the more frequently, before the potential tourist haunt in question is irredeemably ruined – to 'enjoy it before the crowds get there', as the advertisement bids us. As things are then the tourist trade, in a competitive scramble to uncover all places of once quiet repose, of wonder, beauty and historic interest to the money-flushed multitude, is in effect literally and irrevocably destroying them. Once serene and lovely towns such as Andorra[6] and Biarritz are smothered with new hotels and the dust and roar of motorized traffic. The isles of Greece have become a sprinkling of lidos in the Aegean Sea. Delphi is ringed with shiny new hotels. In Italy the real estate man is responsible for atrocities exemplified by the skyscraper approach to Rome seen across the Campagna, while the annual invasion of tourists has transformed once-famous resorts, Rapallo, Capri, Alassio and scores of others, before the last war no less enchanting, into so many vulgar Coney Islands.

None the less the tourist agency continues to conjure up for the young and gullible visions of far-away places, mysterious, romantic, primitive even, to be enjoyed with all 'mod cons' at a cheap package price. Others regard the swelling avalanche of tourists as a great democratic achievement, a unifying force in the world, a growing opportunity for all people 'to see the world and to perceive its life and art'. But, like extending the opportunity to motor into the centre of London to every car-owner in the country, it is a purely illusory opportunity.

6. Over six years ago, a correspondent in the Pyrenees wrote for the *Economist* (22 August 1959) a short piece on 'The Last Days of Andorra'. He observed that tourists still went to Andorra in search of the exotic . . . 'to see its medieval houses and bridges, fine Romanesque church towers and unsullied mountain vistas; to enjoy its eyrie-like calm and pure air. As a result of the tourist invasion, however, Andorra's air is at the moment a nicely balanced diet of exhaust fumes and cement dust, vibrant with the competing *chachachas* of Radio-Andorra and Andorradio; parking is the same kind of problem as in London; and every other beauty-spot is pock-marked with hotels, bungalows and camping sites. One of the loveliest church towers in the country, that at Ordino, has been dwarfed by a grace-less new block sited exactly six inches from it.

'. . . Building sites are being snapped up in Andorra-la-Vella at £25 a square yard. At the present rate of development the whole central valley from Encamp to Santa Julia will soon be one unbroken ribbon of flamboyant façades.'

With slight alterations, this passage would summarize the recent history of hundreds of favourite resorts in France, Italy, Spain, Greece and other Mediterranean countries.

Travel on this scale with the annual need to accommodate tens of millions, rapidly and inevitably disrupts the character of the affected regions, their populations and ways of living. As swarms of holiday-makers arrive by air, sea and land, by coach, train and private automobile, as concrete is poured over the earth, as hotels, caravans, casinos, night-clubs, chalets, blocks of sun-flats crowd into the area and retreat into the hinterland, local life and industry shrivel, hospitality vanishes, and indigenous populations drift into a quasi-parasitic way of life catering with contemptuous servility to the unsophisticated multitude. The issue is not at all that of aristocratic privilege versus democratic freedom, not even that of the genuine connoisseur versus the philistine hordes. Geographical space, the choicest bits of it anyway, forms one of the strictly limited resources of this now tiny planet. And – as in so may other things – what a few may enjoy in freedom the crowd necessarily destroys for itself. Notwithstanding which, under present institutional arrangements (since there is certainly a lot more money to be earned in promoting this process of rapid erosion), unless international agreement can be reached to control further tourist damage our children will inherit a world almost wholly bereft of places of undisturbed natural beauty.[7]

One policy measure alone which would go far to reverse this dismal trend may be hazarded: an international ban against all air travel. With more leisurely travel habits restored – and enforced by prohibiting speeds in excess, say of 30 knots – one could confidently anticipate an enormous reduction in the demand

7. Robert Graves in an extract from his book *Majorca Observed* printed in the *Telegraph* colour supplement (14 May 1965) begins as follows: 'Only fifteen years ago a *New Yorker* cartoon shows an old lady asking her travel agent: "Whatever happened to those nice cheap little islands in the Mediterranean that you used to advertise before the war?" Yet nobody foresaw the brand-new phenomenon of mass-tourism – meaning charter-flights, block-booking of hotels, and so clever a rationalizing of ways and means that a fortnight's holiday would cost no more than an individual return air-fare. This business now brings 5,000 planes a month to a new and vastly enlarged Palma airport every summer, and has encouraged the building of over 1,000 new hotels.'

for foreign travel. With equal confidence one could predict the outcry by the interested parties against the adoption of so drastic ('impracticable', 'irresponsible', 'reactionary') a proposal.

But what is the alternative? To continue to drift along? We have already, and within a few short postwar years, all but destroyed a heritage of tranquil unmarred natural beauty that had else endured the passage of centuries and millennia. With a hubris unmatched since the heyday of Victorian capitalism and with a blindness peculiar to our own time, we have abandoned ourselves to ransacking the most precious and irreplaceable good the earth provides, without thought to the desolation of the future and the deprivation of posterity.

A more diluted version of this proposal, one drawing its rationale from the separate-facilities solution, would be to remove all possibility of swift travel service – which usually means air travel – to a wide selection of mountain lake and coastal resorts and islands scattered about the globe; and within and around them to abolish all motorized traffic. Areas should be set aside for the true lover of natural beauty who is prepared to make his pilgrimage by boat and willing to explore islands, valleys, bays, and woodlands on foot or by horse-drawn vehicles.

Part Three

10

The Myth of Consumers' Sovereignty

So far the critique of economic growth as a social priority has developed within a framework of basic assumptions. In particular, by accepting people's wants as something given to us independently of the workings of the economic system, it is possible to interpret its operation as tending to bring scarce resources into relation with people's wants. Yet within that restrictive framework, and even under ideally competitive conditions, we have shown that any solution which neglects the incidence of external diseconomies may be very far from ideal. None the less, even in the absence of the more conspicuous external diseconomies, once we modify this framework of assumptions to conform more closely with the facts of everyday experience, the rationale of economic growth begins to look very shaky.

The most common of these basic assumptions, one frequently invoked to vindicate economic growth, is that any extension of the *effective* range of opportunities[1] facing a person (whether presented to him through the market or directly by the government) contributes to an increase in his welfare. Similarly any reduction in the effective range of opportunities contributes to a diminution of his welfare.[2]

However, even in a market economy in which government

1. The word *effective* is inserted to indicate that the additional opportunities presented to him are relevant to his circumstances inasmuch as they induce him to select a new combination of goods and services in preference to the old combination which is, however, still available to him.
2. This assumption, equating enlargement of effective choice with improved welfare, is closely connected with the assumption that the consumer knows his own interest best. This latter assumption is one which favours 'free choice' as against 'paternalism' in the distribution of goods. In so far as government taxation (in order to provide goods or services) can be interpreted

intervention is at a minimum, there is one important opportunity that is denied to the customers; that of selecting the range of alternatives that will face him on the market. He can choose only from what is presented to him by the market – and a range of alternative physical environments (mentioned in previous chapters) is not the only thing that the market fails to provide. For one thing, the so-called extension of opportunities is not necessarily *effective*, in the sense defined. When new kinds of goods or new models of goods appear on the market the older goods or models are not always simultaneously available. They are withdrawn from production at the discretion of industry.

The argument purporting to show how consumers' wants ultimately control the output produced is facile enough: for it is, on the one hand, admittedly profitable to be first to discover and cater to a new want, while, on the other hand, it would seem unprofitable to withdraw from the market any good for which the demand continues undiminished. It would not be hard, therefore, to lay down conditions under which the wants of consumers tend quickly to influence the sorts of goods produced. But, unless the wants of consumers exist *independently* of the products created by industrial concerns it is not correct to speak of the market as acting to adapt the given resources of the economy to meet the material requirements of society. In fact, not only

---

as a spending of people's money for them on goods or services that could be produced and/or distributed as economically through the market, one may legitimately talk of 'paternalism'. If the liberal economist ascribes a higher utility to a batch of goods that is freely chosen than to one of the same value that is, to some extent, prescribed by the government he does so on the grounds that a man knows his own interests better than anyone else. The question of the empirical truth of this proposition may be held to be secondary to the political belief that we should act *as if* people did know their own interests best since actions based on other premises would be liable to result in undesirable social and political consequences. It is also possible, however, to regard the proposition as a *factual* assumption about human behaviour – a hypothesis that free choice always, or usually, or sooner or later, brings about a greater access of welfare to the individual than would be obtained under any system that restricted his freedom of choice.

do producers determine the range of market goods from which consumers must take their choice, they also seek continuously to persuade consumers[3] to choose that which is being produced today and to 'unchoose' that which was being produced yesterday. Therefore to continue to regard the market, in an affluent and growing economy, as primarily a 'want-satisfying' mechanism is to close one's eyes to the more important fact, that it has become a want-*creating* mechanism.

This fact would be too obvious to mention, except that its implications are seldom faced. Over time, an unchanged pattern of wants would hardly suffice to absorb the rapid growth in the flow of consumer goods coming on to the markets of rich countries, the US in particular, without the pressure afforded by sustained advertising.[4] In its absence, leisure, one suspects,

3. Admittedly it is difficult in many circumstances to separate the informative from the persuasive elements of an advertisement, to say nothing of gauging the accuracy or relevance of the information provided. 'Smart people smoke Cancerettes!' is a claim which is not easy to test. If we defined the class of smart people we may discover that, in consequence of a prolonged and intensive advertising campaign, smart people have indeed taken to smoking Cancerette cigarettes even though they could not be distinguished from other brands when labels were removed. A picture of the product, or the name of the brand, printed without comment may well persuade people to buy more of the product. However, a case for the abolition of commercial advertising does not depend on such a distinction. Moreover, the abolition of commercial advertising cannot seriously be construed as an infringement of libertarian principle.

All that which is relevant in enabling the public to make a rational choice from the range of material goods and services offered by private enterprise may be more economically conveyed by an impartial body of analysts and administrators – an official or semi-official Consumers' Union in fact. One great argument in favour of this solution is the large saving in resources, both those expended by commerce (much of it in 'counter-advertising') and those wasted by the public as a result of unsatisfactory choices.

4. The view that commercial advertising lowers the price of newspapers and journals deserves a comment. In the last resort the full economic costs of newspapers have to be borne by the public at large. But whether they end up paying for a larger part of the newspaper through their purchases of the goods that are advertised, as at present, or whether, as an alternative possibility, they pay the full cost of the newspaper, free of commercial

would be increasing faster than it is. National resources continue to be used to create new wants. These new wants may be deemed imaginary or they may be alleged to be as 'real' as the original set of wants. What cannot be gainsaid, however, is that the foundation necessary to enable economists to infer and measure increases in individual or social welfare crumbles up in these circumstances. Only as given wants remain constant and productive activity serves to narrow the margin of discontent between appetites and their gratifications are we justified in talking of an increase of welfare. And one may reasonably conjecture that unremitting efforts directed towards stimulating aspirations and enlarging appetites may cause them to grow faster than the possibilities for their gratification, so increasing over time the margin of social discontent.

Be that as it may, in high consumption economies such as the United States the trend is for more goods, including hardware, to become fashion goods. Manufacturers strive to create an atmosphere which simultaneously glorifies the 'pace-setter' and derides the fashion laggards. As productivity increases without a commensurate increase in leisure the accent shifts ever more stridently to boost consumption – not least to boost automobile sales although cities and suburbs are near-strangled with traffic – in order, apparently, to maintain output and employment. The economic order is accommodating itself to an indigestible flow of consumer gadgetry by inverting the rationale of its

---

advertising while paying less for goods no longer advertised, is mainly a question of distribution. If we ignore the costs of real resources used in advertising – the services performed by advertising agencies, additional newsprint, etc. – it is purely a question of distribution; those people who buy more of the advertised products effectively subsidizing those newspaper readers who buy less of them. Once the real resources used up in advertising are brought into account, however, the public is paying more for both advertised goods and newspapers combined than it would pay for them in the absence of advertising.

The contribution of advertising, in terms of 'information' and 'entertainment' currently provided to the public, is not large relative to the resources used. Certainly the flow of relevant and impartial information could be multiplied and made available to the public for a fraction of the resources currently employed in the advertising industry.

existence: 'scarce wants' have somehow to be created and brought into relation with rising industrial capacity.

Under such perverse conditions growthmen may continue, if they choose, to so juggle with words as to equate growth with 'enrichment', or 'civilization', or any other blessed word. But it is just not possible for the economist to establish a positive relationship between economic growth and social welfare.

11

Institutional Constraints on Choice

SINCE economists make rather free with the word 'choice', the reader may excuse some rather obvious remarks that serve to remind us how existing institutional restrictions influence and, indeed, reduce effective choice.

Over the decision most vital of all to his well-being, the epoch and society wherein he lives, the individual alas is unable to exercise any choice whatsoever. Born into a certain social and physical *milieu*, born into a certain home, much of the pattern of his life follows as a matter of course. Many of the consequences that arise from nature and nurture, from inherited natural endowments and from upbringing, he will be powerless to influence. Within limits determined by these consequences he is, later, free to choose an occupation but, having adopted it, the material choices that he exercises through the market are thereafter somewhat narrowly conscribed. If, for example, he becomes a stockbroker or bank manager in the City, his choice of clothes, car, residence, even his choice of food and entertainment, will not differ markedly from that of his colleagues. The conventions followed by friends, associates, and customers will continually weigh with him unless he is ready to forfeit their good opinion of his character and soundness upon which his success depends.

Such trite observations take on significance as the cost of keeping in fashion increases with economic growth. Women's fashions are only a more familiar case in point. Popular articles assert that women positively enjoy being in the fashion – though their pleasure, one imagines, may sometimes be traced to a dread of being seen out of fashion. But for most women it would surely be less costly and less exacting to be subject to fashions that changed less frequently. The choice of the pace of fashion, surely a crucial choice, is not open to the individual, only to society as a whole where, at present, it is left entirely to commercial interests to exploit to the limit of technical feasibility. The fashion industry is the prime example of an activity dedicated to using up resources, not to create satisfactions, but to create dissatisfactions with what people possess – in effect to create obsolescence in otherwise perfectly satisfactory goods. Though it has been doing this for ages, it is the increasing frequency of fashion change, and its extension to many articles other than clothes, that is disturbing. Following the lead of United States manufacturers, we are extending the pace of fashion to automobiles, furniture, hardware and electrical goods. Any practical proposals to regulate the rate of change of fashion in clothes and in durable goods may attract a great deal of public support. The would-be pace-setters would, of course, be deprived of approved opportunities for self-display, but the potential saving in national resources should more than suffice to compensate them.

Turning to the range of goods in the economy, though producers use up resources in creating markets for their goods, they are not permitted to produce any goods they wish for which a market might be created. Existing institutions place limits also on the kinds of goods that will be demanded. A wide variety of drugs, weapons, pornographic literature and entertainment, at present illegal and therefore costly, would be readily available at competitive prices in the absence of existing prohibitions. Men and women might agree to sell themselves or their children into slavery for certain tangible benefits if the law permitted the institution. In a country having a conscript army, the government would have no difficulty in promoting a flourishing market in draft tickets, the richer young men effectively buying their way out of national service to the ostensible benefit of both buyer and seller. Again, if speed limits on our roads were limited to a maximum of 15 miles per hour people's choices would change radically not only in respect of automobiles used, and mode of travel, but also in their choice of residence, in their use of time, and in our design of towns and cities and roads. If the penalty for accidentally killing pedestrians were not merely a fine, as at present, but hanging by the neck, one could predict with confidence a vast change-over to public transport, a voluntary though drastic diminution of speeds, and a quite magical reduction of deaths through traffic accidents. Too much attention has been paid to the concept of expanding choice and too little to the power of continuously changing legislation in altering, for better or worse, the kind of choice that people make.

Finally, let us turn to the restrictions placed on a man's choice of occupation by existing technology and institutions. In seeking to establish the optimal properties of a perfectly competitive economy the traditional liberal economist would argue that just as the individual chooses, as consumer, to buy various amounts of the goods offered by the market, so also, as the owner of productive services, he is guided by market prices in offering various amounts of his services in different occupations. This symmetry is obviously forced on the analysis in the interests of elegance and mathematical convenience. It may be that in some imaginary economy a person could spread his work among a variety of occupations on the familiar equi-marginal principle in the same way as he is deemed to spread his income among the goods offered to him by the market. But modern industry is not so accommodating, and for the superficially good reason that if a man were allowed to choose in this way – choosing each day to put a few hours in this occupation and a few hours in that – the productivity of the economy could not be maintained. The employee has therefore to choose his work subject, for the most part, to the condition that he conform exactly to the working week of the firm.

In the narrow growth sense, one in which social welfare is measured directly by output, such a constraint on working hours may appear necessary. But if the economist is interested in social welfare rather than in physical output he must concern himself with the burden of this constraint on the worker's choice in a modern economy that is almost wholly consumer oriented – and, indeed, the private enterprise system is generally vindicated by reference to the individual's satisfaction *qua* consumer while neglecting his satisfaction *qua* worker. It is, of course, easy to forget that the individual may have occupational wants independent of technical progress since, over time, he is seen to adapt himself to whatever technological means are available. Though we suppose him, at any moment of time, to have a set of preferences among existing occupational opportunities, there is no use in comparing his preferences between newly adopted and obsolete methods inasmuch as he is rapidly deprived of any choice of the latter. The economist has no means of discovering what changes in welfare, if any, result from a change-over from one technology to another.

Yet something may be said. The tedium of repetitive work in modern industry, even that of watching a screen and turning knobs, is easy to underestimate by those fortunate to escape such tasks. One has only to reflect on the efforts and the expenditure incurred by large numbers of people in combating the monotony of their daily occupation, their growing eagerness to engage in all manner of hobbies in their spare time, their desire to recapture a feeling of craftsmanship or creativity – one has only to reflect on these things to discern opportunities for social gain in making existing industrial arrangements more flexible. Nor need one contemplate a clear choice between the existing highly organized system of production and the extreme alternative of uninhibited choice in respect of hours of work and variety. One need only admit the clear possibility of social gain, after full allowance has been made for the consequent reduction in physical output, of extending to people of all ages a much wider choice in the hours of work, a wider geographical choice in the location of smaller units of industry and, above all, a wider choice in the methods of production. Experiment on such lines is obviously inconsistent with any criterion of technical efficiency: some material remuneration would have to be sacrificed in the conscious pursuit of ways and means of deriving positive enjoyment, stimulation, and companionship in one's daily occupation. Indeed, this proposal may be recognized as an instance of the separate facilities concept for promoting welfare. Not everyone would wish to sacrifice efficiency, and therefore earnings, in exchange for more of these other desirable factors. But there should be enough people capable of enriching their lives by such arrangements to justify the experiment.

Measured by the conventional index of finished goods, the implementation of such proposals may well involve negative economic growth. That an increase in social welfare – an increase in the range of effective choice – may be brought about by negative economic growth may appear paradoxical, if not infuriating, to some growthmen. But that is because they are interested in social welfare only in so far as it seems to justify economic growth, and not the other way about, as they sometimes pretend.

12

The Weak Link Between Expanding
Choice and Welfare

IN the preceding two chapters we assumed, provisionally, a positive connexion to exist between effective choice and welfare, and confined ourselves to revealing some of the limitations on effective choice under existing institutions. We also drew attention to the difficulty of detecting and measuring changes of welfare over time in an economy devoted to altering people's tastes. However, even if tastes remained unaltered over time the connexion between effective choice and welfare is by no means self-evident – at least, not in the affluent society.

In the first place, although the whole range of consumer goods is growing, one of its chief manifestations is the multiplication of brands and models of already popular goods. The task of choosing in a rational way, on each occasion, one brand or model from a bewildering and, indeed, ever-changing array of such goods – that is, to weigh up the relative merits of quality, taste, appearance, performance, longevity, and other characteristics with respect to the range of prices of some several score objects all purporting to serve the same need – would be too time-consuming and too exhausting an occupation even if the entire staff of a Consumers' Advisory Board were placed at the customer's disposal. In the event, there are many things a person buys from habit and much that is bought on the impulse. Nevertheless, in all that involves fairly large expenditure on durable goods, the process of choosing is itself a time-consuming business, one that is not made easier by the trend towards more rapid obsolescence of existing models, and by variations in price at different times and in different places. It may seem, on a superficial reflection, that no person need inconvenience himself if he does not wish to; he can always reach out and take the first thing that catches his eye or he can adhere to his customary brand – if it remains available. One can call this a rational solution if one wishes, but it is one that affords little consolation. As the pace of fashion accelerates, as goods become technically more complex and their variety proliferates, the plain fact is that ordinary people do become apprehensive about the increasing possibilities of choosing the wrong thing.[1] If, therefore, an independent panel were given the task of radically reducing the existing prolific variety of goods on the market to a few clearly differential types of each good, one could reasonably anticipate a saving of time and some elimination of anxiety, to say nothing of a potential decline of manufacturing costs arising from the resulting standardization of products.

If the link between choice and welfare does not already appear tenuous, we can go further. The political philosophy of John Stuart Mill may suggest to some that if a man has a mind to drink himself to death no intervention other than that of per-

1. If, beginning with a situation in which only one kind of shirt were available, a man was transposed to another in which ten different kinds were offered to him, including the old kind, he could of course continue to buy the old kind of shirt. But it does not follow that, if he elects to do this, he is no worse off in the new situation. In the first place, he is aware that he is now *rejecting* nine different kinds of shirts whose qualities he has not compared. The decision to ignore the other nine shirts is itself a cost, and inasmuch as additional shirts continue to come on to the market, and some are withdrawn, he is being subjected to a continual process of decision-taking even though he is able, and willing, to buy the same shirt. In the second place, unless he is impervious to fashion, he will feel increasingly uncomfortable in the old shirt. It is more likely that he will be tempted, then, to risk spending an unpredictable amount of time and trouble in the hope of finding a more suitable shirt.

Even if he does find a more suitable shirt it may not have been worth the time and trouble spent in selecting it. Moreover, in continuing to review his choice in the light of additional variety and additional information, he is not gradually approaching the choice of some ideal shirt. Since fashions are changing, and since his tastes are being influenced by advertisements, the expenditure of time and effort only ensures his appearing in an acceptable shirt chosen from the continually changing variety. In so far as a person's knowledge of the intrinsic qualities of a good, and of its fashion, is limited the growth of variety subjects him to some strain, and possibly to some anxiety.

suasion is called for. It is thought better (in some political sense) that a man act unwisely of his own free will – provided, always, his action harms no other persons – than that he be coerced into a wiser course of action. Without taking issue with this doctrine as a political maxim it should none the less be transparent that in many circumstances some measures of constraint on a man's choice can increase his welfare. To illustrate with a homely example, the concept of 'consumer's rent' may be employed by the economist to measure the *additional* benefit a man enjoys in choosing to smoke two packets of cigarettes a day for the rest of his life compared with a situation in which, say, no tobacco at all were available. Any restraint imposed by government edict or any shortage that reduced his ration – directly or through higher prices – below two packages must necessarily appear as a reduction in his welfare. Yet it is far from impossible that if there were a tobacco famine, or if he were conscripted into some task-force which was sent to a place where tobacco could not be had, the craving for the weed might vanish over time, and the man live to bless the event. He would continue his life in better health, and pocket, than before, and assert roundly that his welfare had been vastly improved by these initially frustrating circumstances. This kind of event may be discussed with a great deal of political sophistication, but whatever is concluded it cannot be denied that a welfare economics based exclusively on free choice within institutional constraints does not recognize the ample opportunities for increasing social welfare by initial departures from the free-choice path. If, for example, television or cinema audiences were deprived for a longish period of the shallow entertainment they have habitually succumbed to, many of them might be expected, after a period of tedium, to develop a taste for more sophisticated programmes, so that if the old shabby fare became available again it would be rejected out of hand.

A short visit to the US is enough to convince one that wealth, competition, and free institutions provide no safeguards against the prevalence of appalling standards not only of environment in city and suburb but also in journalism and broadcasting enter-tainment. The opportunities for increasing social welfare through raising standards of taste and appreciation are not likely to be tapped in a highly commercial society.

Such reflections do not necessarily strengthen the arguments for the institution of philosopher-kings or weaken the arguments for political liberty. But they do serve to reveal the bias of welfare prescriptions that would accept as ultimate data the apparent and existing choices of people as if such choices come into being independently of the economic system. If private enterprise has the freedom to expand resources in influencing the tastes of the public in the interest of larger profits, and if so far it has on balance been successful in influencing them for the worse, there can be surely no objection to non-commercial attempts to influence them for the better. To put the matter more formally, subsidies to agencies that support the arts (beyond the support given by the market) are to be justified by the net social benefits above the costs of such activities. And the opportunity for net benefits of this sort exist wherever such agencies are able to help people to form those habits of taste and discrimination which increase the capacity of aesthetic experience and enjoyment. A prolonged campaign to raise the public's standards of taste would appear to be a far more efficacious way of promoting social welfare than the present unimaginative policy of straining away at 'real' output.[2]

A final weakness of the link between expanding output and social welfare is revealed by consideration of what economists are wont to call 'the relative income hypothesis' – the hypothesis that what matters more to a person in a high consumption society is not his absolute real income, his command over material goods, but his position in the income structure of society. In its purest form, the thesis asserts that, given the choice, the high-consumption society citizen would prefer, for example, a 5 per cent increase in his own income, all other incomes constant,

2. The criteria of good taste and bad does not, in this connexion, pose any formidable problem. Much that is produced for public consumption is incontestably bad by any standards and some of it is excellent by most standards, so that the question of locating the boundary between the two need not bother us for a long time yet.

to, say, a 25 per cent increase in his income as part of a 25 per cent increase in everybody's real income. The evidence in favour of the hypothesis in its purest form is not conclusive but it is far from being implausible, and in a more modified form it is hardly to be controverted. Our satisfaction with many objects depends upon their publicly recognized scarcity irrespective of their utility to us. It is not difficult to imagine the gratification experienced by a person living in a country in which all the other inhabitants are aware of his being the sole possessor of a radio, hi-fi recorder, washing machine and other durables. Nor is it difficult to imagine his great satisfaction, arising from the knowledge of his being the sole possessor of these things, melting away as they become common household appurtenances; indeed, of his gradual dissatisfaction with them as he learns that his neighbours now possess far more advanced models than his own. However, the more truth there is in this relative income hypothesis – and one can hardly deny the increasing emphasis on status and income-position in the affluent society – the more futile as a means of increasing social welfare is the official policy of economic growth.

In sum, facile generalizations about the connexion between expanding choice and social welfare which serve to quieten misgivings about the single-minded pursuit of economic growth are here rejected. The fact that what matters most to affluent-society man is not the increase of purchasing power *per se* but his relative status, his position in the income hierarchy, robs the policy of industrial growth of much of its conventional economic rationale. In part, this attitude of affluent-society man is to be explained by the central thesis of this volume: that beginning from the norms of postwar affluence economic growth has failed to provide men with additional choices significant to his welfare; that, indeed, it has incidentally destroyed some cardinal sources of welfare hitherto available. The bewildering assortment of gadgetry and fashion goods offers the sort of expansion that is as likely to subtract from than to add to his welfare. As producer, affluent man has little choice but to adapt himself to the prevailing technology; no provision is made by industry enabling him, if he chooses, to forgo something in the way of earnings for more creative and enjoyable work. Nor, as citizen, has he yet been presented with the vital choice of quieter and more human environments, free of the ravages of unrestrained traffic.

*More Intimate Reflections on the Unmeasurable
Consequences of Economic Growth*

a. Introduction

I

THE clichés that come jingling towards the end of the company
director's annual address about the company's unwavering belief
in economic progress (to which the company makes a modest
contribution) and its power to make the world a richer, more
varied, and more 'exciting' place to live in, have already been
subjected to some buffeting in the previous pages. What slender
links remain between economic growth and social welfare must
now come under further strain as we remove some of the pegs
from the framework of analysis familiar to economists.

The old-fashioned economic law of eventually diminishing
marginal utility was founded on the supposed satiation of human
wants, whether the wants were physical, intellectual, aesthetic
or emotional. No matter how rich he becomes a man has still
but one pair of eyes, one pair of ears, one stomach, one sexual
organ, a single brain and a single nervous system. In the face of
this unremarkable fact of life, continuous material growth cannot
be sustained by a system geared simply to producing ever larger
quantities of the same goods. Hence the importance of product
innovation. New and more expensive goods and services continuously supervene. And in the endeavour to ensure that men
change their wants as rapidly, the economic system must be no
less adept at creating dissatisfaction. Its success in this respect is
symbolized by the postwar emergence of the 'pace-setter' – an
ideal type, hyperconscious of being in the van of fashion, and
imbued with the new virtues of 'dynamism', expertise and unlimited ambition. The more affluent a society the more covetous
it needs to be. Keep a man covetous – 'achievement-motivated'

is the approved term – and he may be kept running hard to the last day of his life.

But for what? Indeed, it is not so much the belief that there must be some hypothetical limit to a man's capacity for enjoyable experience that is pertinent here. I should think that today man is far removed from such a limit. What is pertinent is whether by pursuing material growth he tends, on balance, to converge towards this limit or, on balance, to move away from it. However we determine, there is unmistakable evidence that much of the enjoyment of life still attainable is being marred by a chronic restlessness to realize something bigger and better. Yet there are no circumstances which suggest that for today's *bon vivants* the experience of life as a whole is any richer than it was for yesterday's *bon vivants*, a sceptical view of things no less applicable to the future. That new opportunities, such as visiting the moon, exploring the oceans, travelling at unimaginable speeds, gazing at three-dimensional television screens, using visual telephonic communication, pressing buttons on miracle computers, raising of test-tube babies, and much more besides, will all be available to our grandchildren – if the world survives – need not be doubted. What is to be doubted surely is whether, after their novelty has worn off, the experience of these things can be counted on to deepen the enjoyment of life in comparison with the life people have been leading in different periods and in other civilizations.

One may ride roughshod over a multitude of doubts to a brave tattoo on the theme of the 'infinite adaptability' of man. But the fact remains that man's bodily chemistry, his basic instincts and emotional needs have not, as yet, been altered. Sheer force of will and intellect may, for a while, enable him to act so as to appear to be adapting himself to, and coping with, a physical environment that changes more rapidly each year, but there is much in the rest of his being that will continue – until science can alter it – to protest at the growing stresses to which it is subjected. Thousands of slaves were sacrificed in the building of the pyramids of Egypt. Today we are our own task-masters, dedicating our lives to erecting pyramids of material achievement.

Immersed, as we are, in heaping Pelion on Ossa we pay no heed to the latent antagonisms between the demands of an advanced technological civilization and the demands of man's instinctual nature. In the ruthless transformation of our planet home – the only planet, incidentally, we can comfortably live on – we are concurrently destroying much that man's nature doted on in the past: a sense of intimately belonging, of being part of a community in which each man had his place; a sense of being close to nature, of being close to the soil and to the beasts of the field that served him; a sense of being a part of the eternal and unhurried rhythm of life.

It would be as untrue to assert that in all past civilizations a feeling of security and contentment were experienced by all families as it would be idle to deny that many suffered from hardship, disease, and poverty. But wherever people lived comfortably, whether in town or village, or farm, their satisfactions were rooted ultimately in their closeness to each other and to the natural order of their lives.

II

We shall not, however, pursue this train of thought here, since it is no part of our plan to reconstruct a faithful picture of the world we began to lose in the nineteenth century. Rather, we shall confine ourselves in the following pages to consider the ways in which the organized pursuit and realization of technological progress themselves act to destroy the chief ingredients that contribute to men's well-being. This last sentence suggests the justification for including the present lengthy digression. The reflections, of their own, have no pretensions to novelty: reflections of a similar kind, though more subtly or more forcefully expressed, may be found in memoirs, novels, essays and in literary journals. Those elaborated here, however, claim to be relevant to the costs-of-growth thesis. Thus the suggestion that many of the less congenial aspects of life today are not just a passing phase, an unnatural prolongation of some freak of fashion, is neither original nor interesting. Any statement about such aspects must be more specific if it is to have any claim on our attention. Hence the attempt in the following pages to reveal a clear connexion between the symptoms of social malaise and the processes that are generated by economic growth.

I must confess, however, that I have failed to discover any central theme about which these non-formal considerations might be made to cohere in some simple pattern. Sustained cogitation might eventually disclose one. In the meantime I have grouped the variety of considerations under several main headings and ordered them in roughly ascending importance – the remarks on the cult of efficiency, which close the digression, carrying the gravest implications for social welfare. The sections on profit propelled growth form a digression within the main digression. They discuss some of the disruptive developments brought about by commercial enterprise in a wealthy economy, developments that are not unavoidably associated with technological advance. For what the distinction is worth, they are not therefore so 'inevitable' as are the others treated in the digression.

The question of 'inevitability' requires, perhaps, a further word of explanation. The strictly pragmatic reader, patient enough with arguments critical of the present dispensation so long as alternative dispensations are available, may begin to demur as he reads on. For granted that on balance the unmeasurable consequences of economic growth are unfavourable to social welfare they are, apparently, inescapable. For better or for worse we are wedded to technological advance which, for all practical purposes, is 'built into the system'. Not all readers are pragmatists, however. If the arguments are, in the main, valid, the connexions between economic growth and, for instance, social disintegration are surely of interest to many people. Moreover, if the public are eventually convinced of these connexions, their response need not be ineffectual. At least disappointment is avoided if they remain sceptical of measures that depend chiefly on improved material conditions. More important, people can reject the conscious pursuit of economic growth as a prime end of economic policy. They can cease clamouring for more science and more industrial investment, and turn their attentions instead to more specific measures for adding an increased margin of ease and pleasantness to their brief sojourn on this earth.[1]

1. The question, which age offered to the common man a greater sense of fulfilment, though difficult to determine is far from being either meaningless or irrelevant. But even if there were, on balance, a presumption in favour of the present, it would be *à propos* in this essay to draw attention to some of the more vital aspects of older societies that have crumbled before the advance of technology.

It is impossible, today, to single out any favourable features of a bygone age without inviting the charge of 'romanticizing the past', whereas it is much easier in fact to fall into the opposite errors of romanticizing the present or presenting too gloomy a picture of the past.

Every age has a tendency to interpret history in the light of its own institutions and achievements, if only because time is unidirectional: all past history is seen as leading up to the age in question. And while hindsight exposes the follies of our ancestors, we must depend upon humility to persuade ourselves that our behaviour is no less irrational than theirs. The professional historian, with a disciplined imagination, has difficulties enough in appreciating how people actually felt about the things they said and did. One can expect less of the ordinary reader of history who is easily misled by the propensity of the modern author, eager to engage the interests of a wide public, to reinterpret the past using the idiom, the metaphors, and the analogies of the present.

Even greater errors of interpretation are committed in reaching general conclusions about the quality of life in some past epoch by inter-temporal comparisons based on those features of life on which the present, not the past, lays the greatest emphasis – features that are, indeed, sometimes outside the range of the experience and expectations of our forbears: high and rising material standards, for instance, or hygiene, or 'glamour', or mobility, occupational, social, and geographical. Again, looking beyond the 'industrial revolution' – which was, by almost any standards, one of the worst times of history for the working masses – and contemplating the long hours of physical toil endured in earlier ages (at certain times of the year at least) the modern man may well be appalled. For he lives in a society that is straining its ingenuity to enter the millennium of effortless living. Yet there is no evidence that hard work as such was resented. Provided land was plentiful relative to population, vast inequalities of wealth and station, which appear intolerable to the modern mind, were accepted as part of the eternal nature of things – and a man's personality today must be narrowly in tune with the times if he cannot conceive that an unquestioned acceptance of one's place in the social hierarchy may be more conducive to a carefree spirit than a compulsive striving for status in a competitive and rapidly changing economy.

We look with harsher eyes on the record of persecutions, cruelties, and dangers spread over the past than we do on those that have become a part of the familiar scene. Yet if by Divine interposition, a sixteenth-century yeoman, say, were enabled to read through the newspapers of the last fifty years, what would he think of the methods used and the casualties inflicted in two world wars, and a score of others also? Would he compare the Gestapo so favourably with the Inquisition? Confining ourselves to 'peace-time' would he envy the masses of people vainly trying to find a quiet place to live? What would he think of the time taken to get to work and back each day? Or of lifetimes spent in desperately scrambling ahead? What would be his response to newspaper reports of sex maniacs, arson, drug addiction among the young, growing juvenile violence, race riots, or the hundred thousand killed and maimed yearly in this country alone by their own countrymen in the pursuit of the pleasures of private motoring? Would he not shudder at what he read, and seek to influence the Almighty by prayers and fasting to spare his descendants from a fate so vile?

b. The Growing Menace of Obsolescence

I

THE appearance in history of mercantile societies is associated in the popular mind with the growth of the arts, philosophy and literature. Yet only with the advent of modern industrial societies does it become possible to offer to all men those material and educational opportunities undreamed of in pre-industrial civilizations. The path of progress has not always been smooth, however, and modern history books are seldom at a loss for examples of benighted resistance to technological innovations by ordinary people apparently deficient in historical vision. Indeed, any number of economists can testify today to uphill struggles undergone to induce native populations in economically backward regions to forsake the methods of their forefathers and to come to terms with the notion of efficiency. For one of the prerequisites for the so-phrased 'take-off into self-sustained economic growth' is the collapse of traditional values and the growth of dissatisfaction with the *status quo*.

In so far as the traditional mode of life was indeed deficient in variety and opportunity, dissatisfaction with it is not to be deprecated. What the modern world tends to forget, however, is that dissatisfaction with existing circumstances too easily becomes a habit of mind – a by-product of the commercial society that brought it into being and a condition for the advancement of that kind of society. Bernard Shaw put it succinctly in calling discontent the mainspring of progress. And if, as so many of us seem to believe, progress is to be regarded as *the* social priority, then such costs as are incurred in its promotion are incidental and secondary in importance. Even if some of the unhappy consequences are all too evident their imponderable nature tells against them. For this is a scientific age, and what cannot be measured is not to be reckoned with.

Be that as it may, I shall go on to indicate several additional considerations, too easily brushed aside, that are closely connected with the phenomenon of unabating material progress. First, that it is hardly possible to move along this golden path of self-perpetuating economic growth without subjecting people to manifold pressures, pressures that appear to increase both with the stage of economic growth and with the rate of economic growth. While it is true that a great deal of anxiety about the morrow was prevalent in previous ages – and for many good reasons; fear of famine, of plague, or of unemployment – it is less excusable in the wealthy societies of today in which (excepting the hard core of poverty) material well-being and medical attention are assured for the mass of the people. For all that, whether viewed as producer or consumer or social being, few men today can say that they live, in this age of accelerating change, without any awareness of anxiety.

The status, if not the earnings, of the professional man, the scientist, or the university don, has never been higher. To all appearances, his position is comfortable and secure. Yet today he has to keep up with a quite unprecedented flow of highly technical literature in his field of endeavour. He may, especially if young and impressionable, react to this sort of strain by talking about the 'exhilaration of modern life' or the 'challenge of living in an age of continuous change', but unless he is outstandingly gifted, he has no certainty from one year to the next of being able to cope with technical developments that come at him thick and fast. If the pace is not too gruelling this year, it may well be so next year, or the year after that. The penalty of slipping behind, or of falling out of the race, may be the forfeit of all that he has struggled to achieve and to hold on to in a competitive society – prestige, position, the recognition and companionship of colleagues; the things that buoy him up in an ocean of anonymity.

For the workman, skilled or otherwise, the pressure to keep abreast of technical developments may be slight in comparison but his anxiety is also provided for. Gone are the days when a man, qualified to be a master of his craft, ceased his climbing, stepped on to the plateau, his place recognized and secure in the community he served. There were trials a-plenty in a man's life, but there was not the fear that any year might see him undone and the skills by which he lived, the source of his pride and satisfaction, fall into desuetude. With the trend, however, towards rapid changes of demand, and, more important, rapid industrial innovation, it needs more than the power of his union, more even than the power of the welfare state, to afford a work-man any assurance about his future. Skills painstakingly acquired over many years may become obsolete in as many months. And it is not earnings alone that matter to a man. High unemployment pay and retraining opportunities do not suffice to compensate him for losing his position in the hierarchy of his chosen occupa-tion, for seeing his hard-earned skill and experience thrown on the mounting scrap-heap of obsolete tools.

Since change today is faster and more thorough than it was, say, a generation ago, and a generation hence will be faster yet, every one of us, manager, workman or scientist, lives closer to the brink of obsolescence. Each one of us that is adult and qualified feels menaced in some degree by the push of new developments which establish themselves only by discarding the methods and techniques and theories that he has learned to master.

The same influence operates on a person regarded as a member of the family. Today's young people, those under thirty say, being breathless in pursuit of life-experience and opportunities for status-training are not acutely aware of any hiatus in their lives left by the disintegration of communities, once centred about church and temple, through which people of all ages and circum-stances organized their social activities and become familiar with one another. This lack of a social community will, however, be felt as they move into their later years. Inasmuch as experience counts for less and knowledge, up-to-date knowledge, for more in a world of recurring obsolescence, the status of older men falls relative to that of younger men. And within the family the same force is at work. There was a time, not long ago, when grandparents were, as a matter of course, part of the family circle, and not necessarily an impediment to its activities. Being full of years gave them the right to be heard in virtue of long experience of the ways of the world: the young of all ages might turn to them for counsel, sympathy and affection. The rapidity of change in social conventions and moral attitudes, associated with the technological transformation in the mode of living, renders a person's experience of the world a generation ago largely irrelevant to the problems of the young today. Never was there such a time when grandparents felt quite so useless and unwanted.[1]

Finally, as a consumer, a person's welfare can be adversely affected by continuous product innovation. To have to choose from an ever-swelling variety of products, made possible by intensive advertising, whose comparative qualities and performances are, for the most part, beyond our powers to appraise, can be a tiresome and worrying business. Current analysis of the relative importance of the informative, entertainment, and persuasive elements in any type of advertisement, or statistics of the average degree of success of advertising campaigns, are of little relevance here. It may well be true that few people are actually cajoled or frightened into buying things they do not want, though it may also be true that the very ubiquity and near unavoidability of modern advertising can jar and exasperate. Far more important, however, is its overall influence as an integral institution of the economies of the West. Living in a world saturated with advertisements may well make a man cynical enough to resist the most persuasive selling technique. But though

1. In this pace-making technological civilization the practice is to shunt old people, like obsolete machines, out of the way of today's smaller and more mobile families. And though some of the old are fortunate enough not to have to depend upon their pensions for their material wants, they perforce must suffer emotional deprivation. The growth in separate provision of old people's homes, and old people's flats and villages (considerately furnished with gadgets enabling the infirm to keep house without the help of the young and able), which promotes their isolation from the rest of society – where they are entertained from time to time by social workers and, somehow, jollied along to the grave – may well be the most efficient way of disposing of them. The least that can be said of this form of social vivisection is that it adds to the anxieties of growing old.

he successfully ignores the message of each and every advertisement, their cumulative effect over time in teasing his senses and tapping repeatedly at his greeds, his vanity, his lusts and ambitions can hardly leave his character unaffected. Again, by drawing his attention daily to the mundane and material, by hinting continually that the big prizes in life are the things that only money can buy, the influences of advertising and popular journalism conspire to leave a man restless and discontented with his lot. These influences, moreover, are rapidly producing a society in which standards of taste and of decorum are in a continuous state of obsolescence, leaving fashion alone as the arbiter of moral behaviour.

II

Once we take economic growth to encompass not merely the growth of material goods and services, but the growth also of all the social consequences entailed in rapid technological advance – both the proliferation of disamenities which, as argued, might be mitigated by saner institutions and the less tangible though, perhaps, more potent effects that impair our capacity to enjoy life – there is little one can salvage from the exhilarating vision of sustained economic growth that is suggestive of net social advantage. It might seem reasonable to suppose that although so much expenditure of time and resource goes to producing gadgetry, the small expenditure devoted to cultural subjects is not insignificant when measured in absolute terms. Yet in the atmosphere created by rapid economic growth, an atmosphere in which the 'new' and the 'different' appear as the ultimate criteria, even statistics of cultural advance are suspect. We are told, for example, that out of the 85 million records sold in Britain in 1964, 12 million were of classical music. These figures will almost certainly rise in the near future, but one would be hard-pressed to elicit them as evidence of a cultural renaissance. Any multiplication of this number is obviously consistent with a general picture of a society of determined 'pace-setters'. What surely is relevant are the dominant motives of the record-collectors. And here one cannot lightly dismiss the notion that classical records are for many people tokens of taste and objects of display. It is possible that collectors play their records frequently but with an enjoyment somewhat alloyed by a concern with current vogues in music and sometimes marred by too determined a desire to acquire a musical vocabulary. Sustained economic growth, at least in the richer communities, depends heavily on an atmosphere of being 'with it', and though not all 'with-it' ambitions are unworthy, the more secondary is the purely aesthetic motivation the less intrinsically rewarding is the cultural pursuit in question, whether it be listening to music, visiting art galleries or attending operas. True, one does not have to await the arrival of the twentieth century to find people attending cultural functions purely for reasons of fashion or in order to diversify their repertoire. Novelists throughout the centuries have made merry with such stock characters. But this is neither here nor there in so far as the interpretation of current statistics is at issue. One may safely conjecture that along with the present confused interest in adult education, 'culture', in small packages at least, happens to be currently in fashion. And the swelling sales figures of publishers and record companies are less plausibly interpreted as a mass renaissance and more plausibly interpreted as yet another manifestation of the growing affluence of young 'pace-makers' and 'status-seekers'.

III

The effect of the postwar spread of television is relevant in this connexion. Though occasionally it is agreed that television has destroyed much of the intimacy of family life by funnelling into the privacy of the home the raucous distractions and paraphernalia of other worlds, real and imaginary, it is held, at best, to be potentially an educative force of immense efficacy. The topics discussed by panels of speakers cover morals, politics, science, crime, economics, sex, history, art, music and bringing-up-the-children, enabling the alert public to appreciate all sides of a question. If people do not acquire encyclopedic knowledge – and most of them have forgotten by Thursday what they thought they had learned on Wednesday – they at least acquire an increasing measure of tolerance. Such tolerance, however, is born less of enlightenment than of uncertainty and bewilderment. The repeated re-examinations, for instance, of fundamental questions about religion, ethics, crime, etcetera, with their unavoidable inconclusiveness, serve further to weaken the moral props of an already disintegrating society and to destroy a belief in divinity that once gave hope and comfort to many. The distinctions between good and bad, between right and wrong, between virtue and vice, once held to be self-evident by our forebears, are blurred and reblurred. In consequence, the confidence of ordinary men and women both in their opinions and in their judgements is gradually being eroded, and along with it their self-respect and essential dignity.

What is more, this rapid extension of specialized opinion to every aspect of knowledge and daily living acts to inhibit the spontaneity of a man's thought and expression. Where a century or two ago the ordinary civilized man would speculate boldly on any subject and converse joyfully on all manner of topics, his spirit today is muted in dismal deference to the cumulative discoveries of science and the qualified pronouncements of the experts. His personality shrivels. He has no convictions to sustain him. His discourse perforce becomes restricted to jest, trivial observations, and personal reminiscence.[2]

2. Once one accepts the fact of an advanced technological society, in which television is the popular medium of entertainment and information, any recommendation that certain programmes be discontinued invites the charge of being an enemy of 'The Open Society'. But if one is condemned, one need not remain silent. In so far as liberty is deemed extended as a larger number of people hear a greater variety of views, the only conclusion that follows from the above remarks is that, if true, there can be circumstances in which considerations of social welfare and of liberty pull in opposite directions.

c. Our Shrinking Planet

I

WE do not need the oil companies' advertisements to inspire us to become 'get-away people'. With the unchecked deterioration of environment in town, city, and suburb, get-away people are being provided with more and more to get away from. But where to? When millions are on the move to get away it is unlikely that many will succeed.

One of the paradoxes of our time is that while language is used increasingly to promote expectations of a continuing enlargement of vista– in postwar journalese all discernible possibilities are 'new and exciting', all opportunities are 'rapidly expanding', and life itself is being mercilessly 'enriched' with 'new dimensions of experience', speed barriers, sex barriers, xyz barriers are about to be 'crashed', and scientific 'break-throughs' occur about once a week – there is ample evidence that men are beginning to suffer from a sense of claustrophobia.

An obvious cause of this growing sense of claustrophobia is the rapid development of communications, in particular the continually publicized endeavours to increase the speed of travel. Having succeeded already in moving people through the air at a speed exceeding that of sound, the spirit of progress demands that there be no slackening in man's efforts to bring forward the day when there be no slackening in man's efforts to bring forward the day when we shall sail through space at a speed no less than that of light itself. If it should take us but an hour to reach Hong Kong from London, a further reduction of the journey-time to a half-hour would unquestionably be accepted as an improvement. Yet one of the more manifest and lamentable consequences of bringing places ever closer together in time is that this earth, once thought immense, now seems dwarf-sized. Not so long ago, even a few years after the turn of the century, the world was still a spacious place, a world of vast oceans and continents. Today one has to return to the sea stories of Melville or Conrad to recapture the image of a measureless ocean on which seamen ventured. One could once speak with awe of far-away places reached only by perilous sea voyages stretching over weeks or months; one could speak of distant lands unknown to men, of uncharted seas, of impassable mountain ranges, of fearsome and savage jungles, of coral islands in the South Seas, and enchanting islanders far removed from the corruption of white civilization, of an Africa teeming with wild life and warlike tribes, and of quaint and colourful customs in distant lands as yet unspoiled by modern commerce. True, unless one were a sailor or in very comfortable circumstances, one might never venture beyond the British coast. But for everyone there was still this sense of living in a world of uncountable resources, climates, and peoples, a world of inexhaustible variety and strangeness and colour. Even if most people could only read about, and dream about, sailing off to distant shores, they could yet be hugely fascinated by the tales of travellers returning from places no farther than Switzerland or Spain.

Today, no country is more than a few hours away by plane, and the years will see these few hours whittled down to minutes. Not only will the earth appear to our children as a pitifully tiny affair, it will also appear irredeemably monotonous – so much so, perhaps, that they will seek relief flying through the frozen darkness of space and groping their way over dead planets. We have already spoken of the phenomenal growth of tourism as the most potent factor in the destruction of the earth's dwindling resources of natural beauty. In the attempt to cater for the growing millions of tourists by building hotels, villas, lidos, arcades, casinos, roads, airfields, once dreamy resorts and semi-tropical islands are transmogrified into neon-lit Meccas, agape with jostling crowds and swarming transistorized automobiles.

Any hope of escape far from the madding crowd is, for each of us, flickering out.[1]

And it is not merely the case that our planet is dwindling in size, the differences between places are dwindling also. The annihilation of distance is accompanied by the annihilation of variety. The differences in manners, in customs, in cultures, clothes, food, architecture, differences that once made travel so fascinating an experience are rapidly being extinguished. Fashions in clothes, pop-music, architecture, are becoming increasingly international. Fifty years ago, no more, there were still striking differences between localities in Britain, as much with respect to building as to dialect. Today, one could choose dozens of these new makeshift office blocks to be found in London, or in any other large city, which are in no visible respect any different from their counterparts in other cities from Buenos Aires to Detroit, and from Sydney to Düsseldorf. Of course, there are sporadic efforts to encourage local costumes, music and handicrafts, sometimes for cultural or nostalgic reasons, but more often with a view to encouraging tourist dollars to flow in the required direction. Yet the consummation of this trend in a uniform cosmopolitanism can hardly be far off.

II

One must add to the annihilation of distance and the consequent destruction of variety, the annihilation of time; for a related effect of economic growth, and the atmosphere in which it flourishes, is the psychological imbalance between present and future. Economic growth promotes a predominantly 'forward-

1. At the same time, and in the sacred name of economic efficiency, one of the few peaceful prospects that men still enjoy once the suburbs are behind them; a scene at once familiar, picturesque and reassuring, of cattle grazing on hill, dale and pastureland, is disappearing. As scientists discover new chemicals, a growing proportion of our livestock will never set foot on soil, but will be herded instead into animal factories, there to be blown up to a size and transmuted to a precise texture as quickly and cheaply as is technologically feasible – little thought being spared by the commercial interests involved to the mute sufferings of these hapless creatures.

looking' spirit, one well illustrated by the automobile and oil advertisements with their steely-eyed young executives gazing unflinchingly into the empyrean. Surely no other period in history can have produced perorations laden with such solemnity as 'the future of our children', 'the future of our people', 'the future of the nation', 'the future of our science', 'the future of the free world', 'the future of mankind'. By contrast with this habitual concern with the future, any thought to the present for its own sake must seem improvident, if not vulgar. The more we are conditioned by the Press, by modern business, by scientists, to think in terms of the future, the more indifferent we become to the ugliness spreading about us. The more pie there is in the sky to gaze at, the less attention we pay to what is happening here, on this earth, right now. If we are daily assaulted by the noise of motorized traffic, the perpetual drilling and dust of demolition, we can always turn to the rising statistics of production for consolation.

This fixation on the future enters our lives and affects our well-being in more ways than one. Each of us, in his own affairs, accepts it as the hallmark of prudence to be ever planning for the future, whether we are hoarding money or expertise, building goodwill, seeking promotion, or anticipating a vacation (all too often for the express purpose of restoring our health to enable us to return and perform our daily tasks with renewed efficiency). Our eyes are ever on the clock and our calendars marked for weeks and months ahead. Today's news is barely read before we are impatient of tomorrow's. The very focus of our experience runs ahead of us. The current of events, here and now, passes through us but faintly, so pre-empted are our minds with matters to come.

Thus, the pure taste of the present eludes us. For in this world that we are intent on changing as rapidly as we can, the material advantages are to be reaped by those who look farthest ahead – those who treat the receding present as a jumping-off ground for the future. But this 'futurism', this greed for the rewards of the future, this impatience to realize the shape of things to come, which inspires and fuels the present technological revolution, is just the phenomenon that hastens us through our brief lives and effectively cheats us of all sense of the spaciousness of time. For the art of immersing oneself wholly in the stream of the present is known only to children, and to people living in more settled and traditional societies.

d. Salvation by Science (i)

I

THE image of scientists as a fraternity dedicated to the pursuit of knowledge for the ultimate benefit of humanity is a comforting one. Many a popular book on the scientists of yesterday and today present a picture of men of vision struggling against the prejudices of the age, men from whose inspired theorizing and patient probings into the nature of the universe will come an age of greater glory for mankind. The names of Newton, Pasteur, Mme Curie, Darwin, Einstein, have powerful associations. Not only are they dedicated beings, they are good people, uninterested in the worldly things except for their concern with humanity. They are seen, in fact, as having all the attributes of a priesthood: great esoteric knowledge, immunity from worldly temptations, faith in mankind and prophetic vision.

This popular impression, however, does not stand up to scrutiny. Collective knowledge does indeed continue to grow in extent and complexity, but increasingly it is scattered among the growing army of the learned. In the past, when the world moved at a more leisurely pace and the sum of man's knowledge was substantially smaller, scientists were few in number and their qualifications sprang from genius rather than from arduous or specialized training. Of the scores of thousands of scientists to be found today in all the richer countries only a small proportion can be sufficiently gifted to keep in advance of developments along a broad front of knowledge without strain. For a large number of the fraternity, however, there is nothing for it but to plod along fired by hope or compelled by anxiety. Whether young or old, whether employed in institutes, research establishments or universities, all today are subject to a growing pressure on their time and on their innate capacity in consequence of the sheer output of current research, theoretical and applied. Not only must the scientist strive to keep abreast of the avalanche of journal literature, in which, inevitably, the writing is increasingly concentrated and increasingly technical, if he is ever to achieve some modicum of recognition he must himself contribute a learned paper from time to time to the accumulating weight that is bearing down on·him. Thus, more than other professions, perhaps, the ordinary academic tends to become over-extended, his faculties too polarized to respond fully to other aspects of life, be they intellectual, aesthetic or emotional. Like all too many of us today, he may seek gaiety but is hard put to generate any.

One need not wonder long about how a person of modest abilities becomes a scientist, or a university teacher, at a time when the sum of knowledge is growing apace and at a time when the standards of scholarship are undeniably higher than ever they were. Two factors have made this possible: one is the longer period of training during which the ambitious student tends to neglect all but the minimum of social activity. Indeed, few students come to the frontiers of their speciality before the age of twenty-five and some not before thirty – their more creative years, perhaps, behind them. The other factor is the trend towards specialization. With the increase in numbers working in his chosen field, the specialist sooner or later feels the pinch. Sooner or later his response will be to hive off a smaller segment of the field and devote himself to its more intense cultivation. Close to the frontiers of any subject we shall find thousands of ordinary but hard-working people, each assiduously sifting his own thimble-ful of earth.

This continual splitting and re-splitting of the subject, by which process a myriad of workers may be eventually accommodated over the whole spectrum of any academic discipline, has the unsurprising consequence that only a handful of men know well more than a fraction of the broader discipline in which they work, or are competent to judge the work of their colleagues over a wide field. Editors of learned journals already have difficulties in finding scholars able to appraise the quality of some of the highly specialized papers submitted to them. The postwar trend towards learned papers authored by two, three, four or more names bears further testimony to the growth of specialization and to the difficulties of keeping abreast of the literature in closely related fields. Indeed, such are the demands upon his time and capacity that no scholar is able to read more than a fraction of the output of professional papers in his own field. To quote an estimate made by Professor John Wilkinson, the average scientific paper is read by about 1.3 people – while many are read by several people and a few by hundreds, a large number are read by nobody but their authors (if we exclude the editors).[1] One may well wonder what the situation will be like a generation hence. That our form of civilization will eventually collapse under the weight of the uncoordinated knowledge that is growing, in impressionistic terms, at an exponential rate, is not so unreasonable a hypothesis.[2]

II

Nor does the picture of scientists as a group immune from worldly temptations bear looking at too closely. There is no reason why science and learning should appeal only to the pure in mind and motive. Its prestige has never stood higher – nothing could be more 'in' than science. On the more successful of its devotees it confers not only status but substantial material rewards: even those of modest talents may have profitable associations with government and industry. In the event, scientists have been drawn into the unending scramble for material rewards and public recognition, along with business executives, actors and politicians. A man may be petty, vicious, coarse-grained, paranoid even, and, outside his specialism, thoroughly

1. John Wilkinson, 'The Quantitative Society, or What are you to do with Noodle'; Occasional Paper published by the Center for the Study of Democratic Institutions, USA.

2. What hopes there are for preventing further excessive fragmentation in any discipline would seem to rest partly on increased intellectual assistance from more highly developed computers, and partly on the possibilities of enlarging man's capacities. Chemical means of improving mental performance are in the experimental stage. Advances in genetics may soon enable us to produce super-brain humans.

ignorant, and yet do well enough as a scientist or scholar. He may write a paper because of the intrinsic interest of the problem – indeed, some scientists become so absorbed in problem-solving as to ignore relevance completely – but he is not less likely than any other mortal to become interested in a study that carries with it some sizeable stipend or research grant. Moreover, whatever aspect of a subject engages his attention, he will be spurred on by the desire to 'get a paper out of it'; for the scientist counts his published works as a miser counts his gold. They are his kudos, his claims to recognition. Above all, they are his certificates encashable in the world he moves in.

These observations serve to adumbrate the pedestrian reality behind the glossy captions about 'science in the service of mankind' which herald a prospect of illimitable human benefit from scientific progress. Such captions do, however, express the common faith, a faith shared, needless to say, by the scientist himself. Indeed, the scientist will seldom question the effects, immediate or remote, of his contribution to human welfare. He may assert that increased knowledge of any sort is its own justification. But he is more likely to accept as a self-evident proposition that any addition to knowledge entails an extension of man's power over the universe, an extension of choice and, therefore, an improvement of his lot on earth. And should man not be made happier thereby, should he destroy himself in a nuclear war or corrupt himself utterly, then this surely is the fault of society, not of the scientists – a rather forlorn dichotomy since the scientist no less than the layman is the victim of the misuse of science. Indeed, the response of the scientist to any failure or misapplication of science is the by now familiar one of urging the application of yet more science. If the use in agriculture of certain chemical discoveries is found to have wiped out several species of beings, or to have caused some significant upset in the ecological equilibrium of a region, the scientist can be counted on to remark that more research is imperative. If men and women become increasingly maladjusted in this rapidly changing world of ours, this again calls for more research. Psychologists, neurologists, sociologists, sexologists, will be eager to diagnose these new and fascinating infirmities, themselves the product of technology that threatens to stifle society. The more calamitous the consequences, the greater the challenge. An uncertain picture emerges of applied science carefully sewing us up in some places while accidentally ripping us apart in others.

III

The innocent layman surrounded by a growing array of specialists of all kinds – in the social sciences by economists, sociologists, anthropologists, psychologists and others – is deluded into believing that his welfare is in good hands whereas, in fact, there is no social science expressly concerned with human welfare in the round. In any case, practitioners are increasingly emphasizing 'positive' as against 'normative' treatment in the development of the social sciences; they are concerned, that is, with hypotheses of existing relationships and not with prescription.

In particular, the social scientist is, apparently, a helpless spectator to continued social developments that are fraught with welfare implications. For man's experience of welfare is only to a limited extent influenced by the range of goods placed at his disposal by the economy. The more pervasive influences on his welfare arise from the existing technological conditions. These affect him directly in his capacity as productive agent responding passively to the evolving machinery of industry. They affect him indirectly, though crucially, by their ultimate determination of the matrix of society – by their impress on the shape of the environment, material, institutional, and psychological, which constrains his personality.

But the technological conditions of production are not chosen with a view to enhancing man's experience of life. Nor has any social science the least say in their determination. They evolve solely in response to the requirements of industrial efficiency. Thus, the predominant influences bearing on man's welfare are generated accidentally; simply as a by-product of technological advance. It may well be suspected that the human frame and the human psyche are ill adjusted to the style of living that technology is thrusting upon us, but willy-nilly technology marches on, leaving to the medical profession the unenviable task of dealing with an increasing number of casualties that are unable to cope with the strains and stresses of a rapidly changing world.

In one respect, at least, modern technology could hardly be more ingeniously fashioned than it is for depriving men of the exercise of their character as men. From the beginnings of the 'industrial revolution' men have become progressively more specialized in a narrow range of tasks whether they work in an office, factory or laboratory. Whatever the particular skill employed, all the other qualities of a man, important enough in earlier times – qualities like courage, loyalty, perseverence integrity, resourcefulness, attributes that once entered heavily into his future and into the esteem in which he was held – have begun to lose their value in this unheroic push-button age. In the serious business of earning a living, the other parts of men count for very little. If he were born today, a Robin Hood, a Buffalo Bill, a Clive of India, a Lawrence of Arabia, would probably be a nonentity. There must be, living among us now, tens of thousands of men who in bygone ages would have been glad to venture forth across the oceans, to fight their way through forests, to push back frontiers and to found colonies and settlements, men who in the daily toil and hazard would discover comradeship and vindicate their manhood. Today they must perforce lead obscure and sedentary lives far removed from the restless force of nature, slumped in anonymity, imbibing synthetic visions from the meretricious flicker of a television screen.

Only so little ago as the last war, there were times when the man in uniform could sense the desperate drama in which he was involved. It was possible for people to believe, as they did believe, that the outcome of the struggle depended upon the mettle and morale of their countrymen, whether serving in the forces or in the home front. Men undistinguished in the ordinary business of life learned to live together in mutual tolerance and good humour while subject to a common discipline and to common dangers and deprivations. The friendships that arose in these circumstances were carefree, intimate, and enduring; rare enough in the organized self-seeking of the modern world and hardly to be thought of in the automated civilization of tomorrow. Whatever the toll in the tragedy, whatever the loss of treasure, the poignant and the heroic could not be denied either. But the Second World War is surely the last of the great wars whose outcome will depend upon mass participation. Though for the time being Western countries continue to finance armies of highly trained men, useful enough at present for police action in some under-developed areas, the determining factor no longer lies in the qualities of those who man the guns. The scientist has unavoidably usurped the place and the prestige of the soldier. A push-button war may or may not be in the offing. But if such a war does come, the measure of its horror will reside in the manifest helplessness and uselessness of ordinary men of all ages. Those that die will not be killed in conventional enemy attacks but will be annihilated by the latest products of scientific achievement. They will not die in the battlefield but like rats in a trap.

e. Salvation by Science (ii)

I

NOTWITHSTANDING occasional declarations about its unlimited potentialities for social betterment, science is not guided by any social purpose. As with technology, the effects on humanity are simply the by-products of its own self-seeking. As a collective enterprise, science has no more social conscience than the problem-solving computers it employs. Indeed, like some ponderous multi-purpose robot that is powered by its own insatiable curiosity, science lurches onward irresistibly, its myriad feelers peeling away the flesh of nature, probing ever deeper beneath the surface of things, forcing entry into every sanctuary, moving a transmuted humanity forward to the day when every throb in the universe has been charted, every manifestation of life dissected to the nth particle, and nothing more remains to be discovered – except, perhaps, the road back.

Long before that final consummation, however, we shall learn, too late, that men live not by truth alone, but by myth. Already science has stripped men of the comfort of their most cherished illusions; of the uniqueness of the earth they inhabit, placed in the centre of God's universe; of the immortality of their souls; of the assurance of paradise and life everlasting. In the place of myth, the heroic truths of Science: that man dwells on a small planet lit by an insignificant star somewhere near the rim of an immense galaxy in one of the countless number of galaxy systems scattered through the infinitudes of space; that far from being created in the image of God, and like unto the angels, man has evolved from primeval slime as an accidental by-product of the operation of natural selection; that life itself is but a flickering accident in a measureless universe moving without purpose or destiny.

This, then, is what we are to teach our children. And it is depressing enough in all conscience. Yet the loss for men of the myths and particularly of the great religious faiths, a loss that is the inescapable part of the growth of science, has yet unhappier consequences for them.

It has too readily been assumed by the so-called humanist that men, once shorn of their belief in a higher being, would turn their energies to more worldly things, and their worship of God to love of their fellow humans. The frantic self-seeking for material achievement, being the most glaring social characteristic of those countries that have benefited most from the advance of science, the evidence confirming the first presumption is abundant to the point of embarrassment. But the second presumption, that deprived of God men would turn their love towards one another, is not borne out by the most casual observation. It is not so much that feeling is 'drying up' within us, but that with so much of it being channelled into the aptly-called 'rat-race' – into the pursuit of material success, into the pursuit of new knowledge, into the pursuit of fashion, prestige pastimes, and new sensations – little is left to flow directly between people. Yet the thinner runs this flow of feeling between people the more impatient a man may be to seek immediate relief in the external world of glamour and fashion – a world wherein other people play an incidental role in his schemes of personal triumph, but otherwise do not matter to him.

An age persistently acclaiming its emancipation from imagined Victorian inhibitions about erotic love finds itself curiously uncomfortable in talking about the love of man for his brothers. But the fear of sounding unctuous is itself indicative of the effort required of a generation nurtured, almost exclusively, on material expectations, of opening itself to the experience of affectionate love. Like opening oneself to the experience of God, an act of faith, of bravado even, is involved. For only by disclosing one's vulnerability, and affirming the nakedness of one's dependence upon others, can one cross the threshold from isolation into communion.

It is not surprising then that so many today live immured in themselves, watching helplessly as the days and the years slip by without ever touching the warmth of another human being. The reluctance to acknowledge the full extent of one's need of others is, today, reinforced by those fashionable postures of nonchalance and unconcern. It is becoming harder to resist the temptation to play it safe, to 'play it cool', with the result, inevitably, that one lives it cool, cut off from the inner pulse of life. The belief in a personal God, however, helps a man to come closer to others. Not only does it strengthen his hold on psychic realities in a world frantic with ambitions, the same faith that enables him to open his innermost heart to his Maker enables him also to open it for his fellows.

Only the simple in mind can believe that in the passing away of religious faith humanity has done no more than discarded its primitive superstitions; that a decent community spirit can somehow replace the observances and rituals of religion, and that the moral precepts for a civilized society can as well be founded on the rationality of an enlightened social interest. With the death of God, something in each one of us has died also. In losing a faith that empowered him to surrender to the love and mercy of his Maker, a man lost more than the solace of his faith. He lost that which, by giving impulse to the flow of sympathy and trust within him, led him towards others in the vital experience of love.[1]

1. The common view that cruel wars and persecutions have also been inspired by religious beliefs is too facile to admit as an argument on the other side. Any institution disposing of the immense power and wealth enjoyed over the centuries by the Church could not but tempt ambitious men into political intrigue, corruption and militancy. More important yet, no matter how great the potential beneficence of an idea, it is possible always for men to pervert it to their own interests: every ideology that inspires men can be used also as an instrument of persecution and of conquest by fanatics seeking power. The brave cause of socialism led by Russian revolutionaries issued in an internecine war of indescribable savagery. The cry 'Liberty, Equality, Fraternity', that fired men's hearts, also let loose the horrors that drenched the soil of France in blood. The pursuit of 'virtue' gave Robespierre to history. Napoleon's armies of 'liberation' looted and tyrannized over Europe.

So long as men are ambitious for power, any idea that inspires people will

II

But disencumbering men of their faith in God is not the only service conferred on mankind by science. In so far as men still cling to a belief in their intrinsic value as human beings, the advance of science provides an opportunity of a yet greater act of emancipation.

Sooner, rather than later, we shall be presented by science with the power to determine the sex of the unborn infant, indeed to determine its genetical composition, and to dispose forever with the need of a mother's womb. Already science is opening up for us a wonderland of computers, automation and cybernetics. Almost anything a man can do a machine can do or soon will be able to do at least as well, and infinitely faster. Scientists are at work on machines that translate, machines that write poetry, machines that compose music, machines that learn to play intellectual games like chess, machines that generate hypotheses. Of course, *man* has made these things: we have not quite reached the stage where machines create other machines of their own volition. Let us take what crumbs of metaphysical comfort we can get. For once we turn from *man*, as a metaphorical embodiment of the extent of human knowledge, to ordinary men and women, we have no choice but to realize that in one attribute after another they are being outdone by contraptions of wire and chemicals. Indeed, science is now successfully exploring substitutes for man's internal organs, a project of mercy to be sure, and with the prospect one day of enabling men to free themselves from subjection to the weakness of human flesh. If machines are becoming like men, men are no less determined to become like machines in a most literal sense.

In the meantime and to a rising chorus of hosannas to the miracles of modern science, the layman – and, beside the sum total of scientific achievement, we are all laymen now – becomes, every day that passes, more of a bewildered spectator to what is

be readily exploited in the endeavour to gain the support necessary to wield power. And as with freedom, so with religion one may truly exclaim, 'O God, what crimes are committed in thy name!'

happening around him, willy-nilly having to adapt his mode of living to the technology of industry and to the flow of gadgets on to the market. Flattered by the Press for his readership, wooed by the politician for his vote, cajoled by the salesman for his money, how can he escape the feeling that he is naught but a unit of exploitation, one among millions, and as near anonymous as makes no difference?

As he is shunted into the era of automation and freed further from mental and muscular effort, all the syrupy sounds of television, all the baubles and the paraphernalia of soft living, and all the eupeptic drugs in creation will not suffice to conceal from him the stark facts of his predicament. He may be taught to play games for his health and to seek recreations that soothe his thwarted instincts. But as an ordinary human being the reins will have slipped from his hands. He will live by the grace of the scientist, destined to become a drone, protected for a time by social institutions and the persisting remnants of a moral tradition, but transparently expendable like some thousand million others heaped like ants over the earth.

More Intimate Reflections on the Unmeasurable
Consequences of Economic Growth

f. Profit-propelled Growth (i)

SUSTAINED technological advance, I have argued, tends inexorably to destroy the sources of satisfaction of ordinary people regardless of the form of economic or social organization. It is, however, worth distinguishing certain features common to the affluent West, where economic growth is directed in the main by commercial forces, if only because some of these features have become so marked and, to some people, so manifestly vicious that they are apt to obscure, temporarily, the less immediate but ultimately more destructive consequences associated with technological advance *per se*.

Already we have had occasion (in Chapters 10, 11 and 12) to dismiss as untenable the doctrinaire claims made on behalf of the private enterprise system, in particular the claim that it enhances welfare by extending the range of choices open to society. We now turn briefly to some other examples of the more overtly corrupting influences exerted on society by the ceaseless search for profits in a mature economy.

(1) The wealthier the economy the greater the opportunities for the so-called growth industries. With an increasing margin of expenditure available for 'luxury items', the chance of making a quick fortune by some new article of wear, or some new mechanical gadget, is in the forefront of the minds of business executives and of hopeful young men as yet unplaced in industry. Indeed, some products that are introduced into the economy as novelties or luxury items – the telephone, the private car, the television set, for example – so influence the growth of the economy as to become necessaries for the mass of the people. The rapidity and apparent ease with which anyone acting on a lucky hunch can

become a millionaire has always been played up in the United States, yet never so persistently as today. One cannot easily escape the welter of success stories about people, young and old, educated and semi-literate, who have become wealthy overnight, so to speak, by gambling on a bright idea or by a series of shrewd transactions, honest, shady, or a mixture of both. As an essential ingredient of the contents of newspapers, popular magazines, and television programmes, such tales have become a part of the daily intake not just of the business community but of society at large. It goes without saying that the overnight fortune is less likely to be made by producing some staple item more efficiently than by inventing some 'gimmick', by discovering some new 'need', or by creating some fashion.

The net gains of the fortune-seekers themselves, however, are of less concern to us than the effects on the public at large. The opportunities for quick fortunes, by the successful marketing of novelties and gimmicks, are further magnified in a wealthy economy by the formation of a volatile consuming public severed from the sobering influences of tradition. Indeed, the chief hope of maintaining the economic momentum of a wealthy private-enterprise system lies in the development of such a consuming public. As already indicated, the success achieved in maintaining sales momentum in a wealthy commercial society requires the continuous creation of new dissatisfactions which are made to rise phoenix-like from the ashes of old satisfactions. And this process is facilitated by just such a consuming public, one whose tastes are uninfluenced by traditional notions of excellence and whose acquisitive impulses are unrestrained by any standards of propriety. Thus, taste becomes the slave of fashion, and fashion the creature of profits. The ideal consuming public for the wealthy competitive society is apparently one that is free-floating in time, a public that can be moulded and segmented and pulled hither and thither by bright-eyed ad men. And if this ideal public is, in fact, so conveniently coming into being in economic conditions of near-surfeit,[1] some thanks are due also to the pronouncements

---

1. I have no doubt that redistributive policies would raise aggregate expenditure even in the absence of sales promotion. But it is conventional to

of the technocrats who bid us seek emancipation by embracing the exciting idea that perpetual and accelerating change is the essence of our new civilization, a civilization in which social norms have no time to form and conceptions of right and wrong are functional and ephemeral.

(2) Owing to high employment and postwar affluence, one of the fastest growing markets in the West, just now, is that drawing its substance from the pockets of juveniles. Not surprisingly, the US provides an outstanding example, with the luxury expenditure of American 'teenagers' (between thirteen and seventeen years old) averaging (in 1965) some seven hundred dollars a year. Given spare cash on this scale, one need only bear in mind the impetuousness and gullibility of youth, now exposed daily to the suggestions of teenage magazines and to high-powered advertising media, to appreciate the boundless confidence with which so many businessmen view their future prospects. Using the magic pipe provided by Madison Avenue, private enterprise has taken on a new role as Pied Piper of Hamelin followed by hordes of youngsters jingling their money and tumbling over themselves to be 'with it', without of course the faintest notion of what they are 'with' or where they are going. And it seems scarcely credible that eminent economists on both sides of the Atlantic continue with all solemnity to apply themselves to the study of means whereby national outputs can be expanded more rapidly at a time when so large a portion of any additional output caters to this display of puerile extravagance and frantic go-go.

This new manifestation of commercial growth is not merely outlandish, its repercussions on society are pernicious. For though assertive impulses associated with the process of growing up can admittedly bring about occasional tension between old and young even in stable societies, the differences in outlook between a youth and his father are considerably aggravated by this gathering

accept as a political datum the existing structure of disposable income. With the given structure of distribution of disposable purchasing power, the US is a near surfeit economy in the sense that sales pressure and created obsolescence are necessary to maintain the propensity to spend.

pace of change. Up to a generation ago it was common enough for a young man to forsake his father's gods at some stage in his life, yet he generally managed to do so without estranging himself completely from his elders. Difference of opinion between generations was not incompatible with sympathetic communication between them. If the young rebel forsook his father's gods he generally embraced new ones, and his defiance was tempered by the outward forms of respect for parents so that, differences in opinions notwithstanding, they could still partake in the common fund of affection that unites a family. Today, with the dissolution of a common frame of ethical reference, communication between the generations appears to be breaking down. Contempt rather than defiance has come to mark the attitude of the young towards their elders. After all, what is there to defy, apart from the police, when conventional morality has all but withered away? In a commercialized society in which the most money is made by fanning the flames of minor vices – envy, lust, vanity, avarice – a society in which status and success are the overt rewards of sustained self-seeking, it is no great wonder that utter cynicism is in vogue with the young. In so far as this cynicism breeds among the young a negative couldn't-care-less attitude towards adult approval, they are the more readily exploitable by the commercial purveyors of frippery and feathers.

And never was a younger generation so ill equipped to withstand the siren songs of the entrepreneurs. Nor poverty, nor filial bonds, nor church authority, nor tradition, nor idealism, nor inhibition of any sort stand between them and the realization of any freak of fancy that enters their TV-heated imaginations. Social workers and journalists who have entered the candy-and-tinsel world that teenagers increasingly seek to inhabit, and have witnessed their mawkish raptures, their cultivated gluttony, their drug sessions, and their stylized seductions, are uncertain whether to be appalled or exhilarated by these near-hysterical attempts of the young to divest themselves of responsibility. But the comforting 'frank and free' epithets, with which the imperturbable progressive is wont to dismiss it all, just do not stick. This 'permissive' world that is emerging is not a product of any new

Enlightenment; no ethic or principle is involved; no idealism pervades it. Its genesis is the moral vacuum created by the bewilderment of their parents caught up in a dissolving society. The word, moreover, belies its nature. Inasmuch as it imposes on the young the strain of repressing much of their individuality in the engrossing task of conforming to all the rages of juvenile fashion, it is all but compulsive.[2] For many of these young people only the exacting demands of a competitive and technically sophisticated civilization stand between them and their surrender to the rituals of the new permissiveness.

In such a milieu, no one need wonder that crime, in particular robbery with violence, is one of our fastest growing industries. To the uncluttered conscience of the young, mundane considerations preponderate. These include the fact that the crime industry is increasing in efficiency: the rewards are larger and the chances of being caught smaller; and the fact of a growing public propensity to regard the criminal as the hero rather than the police. And if the deterrents are weaker, the incentives are stronger. The visions portrayed by the glossy magazines of a perpetual *dolce vita* enjoyed by a young, smart, ruthlessly selfish, fast-moving, freely-spending clique act as a standing temptation today to the impressionable young to make good the deficiencies of talent or fortune by crime rather than by industry.

(3) In a centrally controlled economy such as that of the USSR, the rapid spread of higher education in the postwar period has provided people with both a rising standard of consumption, and a dependable and potent source of anxiety. But in a predominantly commercially directed economy, in the US more than the UK, the growth of anxiety among students and parents has become near pathological. Since the entrance to the universities is regarded, not without reason, as the indispensable first step on the ladder to worldly success, and subsequent degrees as

2. Among all too many of the young, sexual experience too has become not merely permissive, it has become mandatory. Nor is it enough merely to make love. It must not only be done but, like justice, it must be seen to be done.

effective passports into the élite occupations of high status and earnings, open cheating during school examinations has become endemic.[3] The response of commerce, with the connivance if not the active support of high schools and colleges, to the fears that afflict a growing number of students could have been predicted: an endless stream of hastily contrived textbooks (most of them directed towards some specific course), of collections of lecture notes (sometimes mimeographed on the campus), of concentrated cram courses in pamphlet form, of paperbacks congested with potted knowledge, and of digests of exam questions complete with model answers.

And why not? American universities are moving with the tide and are on the way to transforming themselves into vast automated degree-punching factories, equipped with computers, closed-circuit television, and rows of teaching machines. At one end of the factory the raw freshmen are sucked in and, with the minimum of human contact, are passed from process to process, imbibing information on the way, regurgitating it at set intervals to be inspected by machines. If not revealed defective they will emerge at the other end, exhausted perhaps, but ready to be stamped with the firm's warranty. Admittedly, much graduate teaching is still in the handloom stage, and the finished product of high technical excellence. None the less, with the inevitable devaluation of the bachelor's degree, and the consequent growth in the population of post-graduate aspirants, one may confidently anticipate some extension of the principles of mass-production to the training courses for higher degrees.

The problems of the staffing of these new metropolitan-type universities appear to be met by adopting methods familiar to such competitive industries as film-making or big league football. Academic stars, too, have become increasingly mobile, tending to move to where the contracts are fattest, or, at least, to those institutes where the tangible advantages are greatest. A sub-

3. According to a report in *Newsweek* (21 March 1966): 'Columbia University's Dr Allen Barton who supervised a study of ninety-nine colleges that concluded half the students in the sample had cheated, believes high school cheating is even more prevalent. . . .'

stantial part of the duties of the senior staff members of American universities consists of organizing appeals for the funds necessary to continue their bidding and counter-bidding for the services of academic VIPs. The effects of this competitive scramble on standards of scholarship and of teaching remain to be seen. One may, however, ascribe to it the growing impatience to have published work to one's credit. But the knowledge that others also are striving to break into print adds further to the pressure to submit one's work the sooner, before it is anticipated by others. The effect of this pressure to 'get in' first, at a time when rapidly increasing technical and specialized knowledge has augmented the difficulties of editing a scientific journal, goes some way to explain the extent of 'premature publication' in journals – the number of papers that are inelegant, unfinished or unintelligible. To this competitive system one may also ascribe a marked preference by competent staff members for research as against teaching, a preference that the university has to respect if it is to be able to attract to its faculties the big names and the promising young men.

These developments, an extension of the market-place, with its truck-and-barter manoeuvres, to the big business of higher education, are a far cry from the traditional conception of the universities as seats of learning. Far also is the current conception of education from that which for centuries inspired reformers and philosophers, that of education as a good in itself; that of education as a source of enrichment of man's personality, inasmuch as it leads to an enlargement of his knowledge, his sensibilities and his intellect. Above all, education was looked to as an influence for bringing people closer together through a common appreciation of history, and of the natural world, and of their heritage of art and literature.

In today's world, prostrate before the notion of economic growth, the idea of education as an end in itself has a distinctly nostalgic flavour. Almost wholly, today, education is thought of as a means to material ends. Adult education is, for all practical purposes, unalloyed vocational training, with the degree associated with it aptly dubbed the meal-ticket.

It may be protested that this feverish postwar expansion of vocational education at least brings us closer to the ideal of universal equality of opportunity. Yet, the nearer we come to realizing this ideal the more closely we approach a fully-working meritocracy: a system of society in which rewards are based ultimately on the manifest inequalities of intellectual and artistic endowment – in effect, then, on pure accident of birth. The culmination of these trends will issue perhaps in a yet more efficient society but hardly a more just society, and possibly one that is a great deal more irksome, indeed mortifying, to the lower echelons than was, say, the eighteenth-century system of landed aristocracy in Britain.

g. Profit-propelled Growth (ii)

(4) ALTHOUGH drawing support from writers and liberals, the steam behind the movement for the abolition of all forms of censorship, and more specifically in favour of complete freedom of erotic subjects, is predominantly commercial. So-called men's magazines and postwar cinema have accustomed the public to tolerate new forms of bowdlerized pornography. The only question now is should the public succumb to the pressure of interested groups – well-meaning liberals as well as Peeping Toms and enterprising publishers – for the removal of all legal restraints.

The arguments for extending licence are not new. Indeed, they are more of historic than of current interest. The popular liberal arguments turn on thin-edge-of-the-wedge themes and on the social or aesthetic consequences of subjecting artistic and literary inspiration to the veto of the authorities. The good liberal will readily admit the possibility of abuses but, he insists, an open society must run such risks in order that artistic expression may flourish and enrich the imaginative experience and thus the lives of its citizens. To the argument that literature is invariably impoverished by any restraint, legal or social, that prohibits the treatment of any aspect of life – a proposition that compels us to ponder on the unrealized potential of a Dickens, a Hardy or a Conrad – we may add the hedonistic view that pure pornography be recognized as an art form that affords pleasure and excitement to some people, and also the therapeutic view (currently, however, in ill odour among psychiatrists) that depiction of sexual extravagances, perversions and cruelties, either in literature or on the stage or screen, tends to air our repressed fantasies, purge us of our tensions, and so improve our emotional health.

These arguments for an extension of licence are somewhat

removed from the realities of the interests involved. None the less, those who accept them ought to recognize the difficulties they lead to. Inasmuch as one or other of such arguments is believed to justify the removal of any particular kind of censorship it justifies also the removal of *all* kinds of censorship. If, in the defence of freedom of expression, it is affirmed that anything done by men or women, or anything thought by men or women, is a part of life, and, *therefore*, a potential art form, we have excluded nothing. If James Joyce is permitted to follow his hero into the toilet so as to reveal certain aspects of his character, what obscene or brutal incidents cannot be absolved on the grounds of character revelation? If any controversial book or play is to be vindicated by its capacity to stir thought or feeling in a man, then again there can be no objection to sexual intimacies performed on the stage if the drama 'calls for it'. Neither can there be any objection to any stage presentation of homosexual, incestuous or other perverse sexual practices, performed in all circumstance and detail. For such a performance would undoubtedly reveal something of the character of the participants and could be counted upon to excite some feelings among the spectators. And what of performances of physical sadism, the exquisite torture of naked bodies, the crucifixion of squealing infants, or any other such inspired scene designed to pluck sharply at the raw ends of our nerves? After all, the resultant excitement, the shock or horror, or savage relish, are all deeply felt experiences – though we must allow for the possibility over time of our appetites becoming jaded for lack of yet stronger fare.

Whatever the answer, the fact remains that until recently private interests were condemned to scavenging odd nuggets of alloyed pornography found lying about the banned entrance to a mine of apparently unlimited commercial potential. It may be a brave gesture to open up the entrance, another challenge maybe. But the result of the experiment, even if not disastrous, is hardly likely to promote the happiness of mankind.

It is idle to pretend that, after passing through a dark period of confused counsels, a more mature society is now attempting no more than to restore to health and freedom natural instincts erroneously repressed. For we no longer live in a stable society, much less a mature one, but a society being rent apart by the torrential forces of modern technology and commerce, and one already torn wide open by modern communications, a society in a state of rapid dissolution. This is not the time to search for lost innocence. It is not as if we are, or could ever be made like, the primitive Tahitian islanders discovered by Captain Cook, who openly enjoyed their sexual activities and found every prospect pleasing. And if we could be, the medium of transfiguration is not likely to have much affinity with those employed by commercial interests. Is it possible for sophisticated people to believe that 'erotic' picture magazines displaying white and black starkness of thighs and wombs, of breasts and buttocks in mammoth proportions, provide nothing but aesthetic and sensuous pleasure to their beholders? Or that the highly spiced sadistic sexual fiction which, even under the present dispensation, finds its way into pulp magazine and paperbacks offers to its readers no more than natural enjoyment. The sad truth is that the vast market for this proliferating pornographica is one of the clearest symptoms of the sickness of society. For complex reasons, associated with the pace and pressure of modern life, all too many adults who find themselves unable to attain ordinary sexual fulfilment are tempted by the new supercarnal erotic art to withdraw further from the potential reality of experience set by biological limitations into the gaping jaws of fantasy, so isolating themselves further from affectionate communication with others.

The movement to legalize pornography is one with the movement to legalize the sale of drugs – and for motives that have little in common with John Stuart Mill's eloquent plea for liberty. In a civilization where sexual frustrations are magnified by a rising tide of commercially inspired and quite unrealizable expectations, such movements gather their force from a desperate search for some magic potion to spark off buried instincts, or some catalyst to cleave open the kernels of sensation.

Alcoholics who cannot resist a drink would be wise to vote for the closing of public bars. In a civilization as vulnerable as ours is to the many corrupting influences of commercial enterprise, we should have the prudence to resist the invitation to 'crash through the sex barrier'.[1]

The last word must be with Plato, a man who was more fearful of corruption through freedom than through tyranny. The good life is the whole life, a harmony, each attribute present in just proportion. Each part of a man's nature can be likened to a musical instrument that has its place in an orchestra. If all play in harmony the tone is rich and musical. If some instruments play too loudly and other instruments are neglected, the resultant sound is harsh, perhaps unbearable.

The rapid economic growth of the West over the last half century and especially the last two decades, has not yet been

1. A time when the study by Johnson and Masters, *Human Sexual Response* (May 1966), is arousing interest among the critics provides an opportunity of expressing doubts also about this approach to the mid-century obsession with sex. If there were no other choice, the recent and engagingly pathetic 'refreshingly frank discussion' phase is to be preferred to the yet more futile phase that would disseminate among the general public the findings of prolonged and detached studies of the physiology of sex. Though it is generally conceded that there may be more in the human sex relation than can be satisfactorily explained in physical terms, and that there are nuances of pleasure and intimacy incompletely revealed by indices of performance and measure of orgasm, the ingenuous liberal will persist in his quest for truth. Why not measure all that can be measured today, and tomorrow we shall measure more? Why not let the light of day into dark places, and so combat error and superstition? Why not, indeed, in this heroic age of barrier-crashing? Yet one does wonder just what extra dimension people hope to discover on emerging. After all, their manifest impatience to break through each new 'barrier' itself arises from the growing frustrations of a way of life that is a by-product of so many other much-heralded break-throughs.

Already we have touched on some of the consequences on our lives of being deprived of the warmth of myth and mystery by the advance of knowledge. In so far as knowledge supplants spontaneity it also reduces the intensity of a man's experience. Detailed contemplation of the particular ways in which our reflexes function is more apt to hinder than to help them. If we think too closely about the process of absorbing information from, say, the act of reading a book, we will find it harder to continue the process. By trying to watch ourselves thinking, the thinking itself falters to a halt. An inescapable consciousness of the phases and chemistry of the sexual act must serve also to weaken its spontaneity and to qualify that surrender to the upsurge of feeling necessary for its fulfilment.

accomplished without traumatic effects on its populations. Tension is everywhere more evident than harmony, disproportion more evident than proportion. The gross overdevelopment of the acquisitive instinct has its genesis in the industrial free enterprise system of the Classical economists. The increasing obsession with sex, and with sexual display masquerading as fashion; the technique of distilling the carnality of sex, as though it were an essence to be poured lavishly into all forms of modern entertainment, these too owe much to private enterprise and advertising. The result, today, with commerce eagerly reacting to the expectations of excitement it has done so much to create, is the gross displacement of a social libido. And there are no countervailing forces at work today to coax it back into a proper scheme of things. Since there is no road back there is, alas, the undeniable inclination to move 'forward'. Indeed, with the Church in disarray, with the 'experts' divided and the public perplexed, it is not to be expected that the law will hold out much longer against the mounting commercial pressure, backed by naïve writers and liberals, to abolish all forms of censorship leaving a morally fragile and edgy society to cope with the flood as best it can.

More Intimate Reflections on the Unmeasurable
Consequences of Economic Growth

h. The Cult of Efficiency

I

WE have already indicated in an earlier chapter that the concept of expanding choices has little application to the range of opportunities that face working men. The loss of aesthetic and instinctual gratification suffered by ordinary working men over two centuries of technological innovation that changed them from artisans and craftsmen into machine-minders and dial-readers must remain a matter of speculation. It need not, however, be supposed that every phase of this historical transformation produced a change for the worse: it may well be that, beginning from some period in the first half of the nineteenth century, the conditions of work have been steadily improving. Yet the conditions of work, including the social facilities provided, may not be the chief factors contributing to the satisfaction derived by men from their daily tasks. It is more than just possible that the chief source of men's satisfaction resides in the kind of work they are called upon to perform and on the regard in which the product of their work is held by their fellows. Two centuries ago, before the 'industrial revolution' was properly launched, a skilled workman in this country was a craftsman. Whether he worked in wood, clay, leather, stone, metal or glass, he was the master of his material, and the thing he produced grew in his hands from the substance of the earth to the finished article. He was ever-mindful that he was a member of an honoured craft; that he had reached his position after a long apprenticeship; and he took legitimate pride in the excellence of his work.

We are far removed today from that state of society in which craftsmen worked with their own tools in transforming the material into the finished product. And though few workmen alive will have known a situation when it was otherwise, it does not follow that no loss is experienced. Certainly those who have lived through the transitional phases have borne eloquent testimony to their misgivings. Leaving aside such episodes of open resistance to technological improvements, there is no lack of expressions of sadness and regret in the English literature at the passing of the skilled hand-worker. One that comes to hand is the touching lament reproduced from George Sturt's *The Wheelright's Shop*: 'Of course wages are higher – many a workman today receives a larger income than I was ever able to get as "profit" when I was an employer. But no higher wage, no income, will buy for men that satisfaction which of old – until machinery made drudges of them – streamed into their muscles all day long from close contact with iron, timber, clay, wind and wave, horse-strength. It tingled up in the niceties of touch, sight, scent. The very ears unawares received it, as when the plane went ringing over the wood, or the exact chisel went tapping in (under the mallet) to the hard ash with gentle sound. But these intimacies are over. Although they have so much more leisure men can now take little solace in life, of the sort the skilled handwork used to yield them. Just as the seaman today has to face the stokehole rather than the gale, and knows more of heatwaves than of sea-waves, so throughout. In what was once the wheelwright's shop, where Englishmen grew friendly with the grain of timber and with sharp tools, nowadays untrained youths wait upon machines, hardly knowing oak from ash or caring for the qualities of either.'

The growing popularity of do-it-yourself kits and craft hobbies is evidence surely of a search to recapture something of the deep satisfaction enjoyed by the craftsmen of old that comes of mastering the material and creating with the hands. The pity of it is that such hobbies can be enjoyed only briefly after the day's work, or at week-ends, instead of being the daily work itself. Of course, we are assured by the technocrats that once we reach the promised land of Newfanglia the opportunities for leisurely enjoyments – at least in the 'long run' after all the initial economic disturbances have been overcome – will be immense. To the engineering cast of mind, work, any kind of work, is input only; it is the effort expended in producing output. Since *all* input is regarded as a 'disutility', and *all* output as a 'utility', efficiency consists of reducing the ratio of input to output. If the engineer is able to 'lighten men's toil' to such a degree that the 'curse of Adam' is effectively removed, then surely man is forever freed from the daily grind. He need only do the sort of work that interests him, and then only when he feels the inclination. Surely a dazzling prospect for man!

But what of the innate needs of ordinary men? It is not just a question of the limits to leisure that can be enjoyed: few of the rich, in fact, devote themselves full time to the hectic pursuit of pleasure. Many of them adopt causes, or continue to engage in empire-building of sorts: for most men need to feel that their work matters to society – a need that is harder to fulfil as society becomes increasingly more impersonal. The creative satisfaction enjoyed by the craftsman of old, critical though it was in the pattern of his well-being, did not of itself suffice. Social recognition of his work must be added thereto before his contentment was assured. If a master-baker, displaced by the invention of completely automatic ovens, were so fortunate as to be compensated with a sum of money enabling him to buy a set of his old-fashioned ovens and withal to live comfortably, though he could now continue to bake his five hundred loaves a day, he would be unlikely to continue it as a hobby. What he creates as a hobby may well be an excellent thing, or it may not be. His friends may admire it or they may just be polite about it. But whatever their response, it is plain enough that it does not matter very much to others whether he continues or discontinues with the work. And this is a fact that makes all the difference to the basic self-respect of our displaced baker. Even a great artist will not escape a feeling of bitterness if society pays no heed to his work. And the ordinary worker stands in need of more re-assurance than the great artist. For the craftsman who produces directly for a community that both appreciates and needs the product of his hand and brain, and evinces that need by a readi-ness to pay for his skill, there is that blessed feeling of belonging and of being an indispensable part of the daily life of his com-munity. Whatever else may have been lacking in that smaller scale of society in which the yeoman tilled the soil and masters and apprentices worked with patient skill at their craft, there was always this unassailable self-respect and, therefore, that abiding sense of security which is no common thing in the feverish jostling world of today.

And not only a sense of our own worth but a sense of the worth of others is being lost in pursuit of efficiency. The more we become fascinated with the measurable aspects of human achievement the easier it is to slip into a frame of mind that judges people according to numerical systems and that ranks their worth on some scale of efficiency. In time we lose sight both of the subtle and engaging facets of the character of each individual and of the intrinsic value of each human life. In continually directing our calculations to the uses of other men, regarded as means to the attainment of material ends, the modern world's preoccupation with efficiency tends to blunt our moral sensibilities.[1]

II

There are other vital sources of gratification, equally unmeasurable by the engineer's yardstick, that are being lost in the obsessive scramble of the rich countries to exploit technological opportunities. For many of the incidental consequences of the mode of production which technocrats, in their overriding task of spreading innovation and increasing efficiency, would regard

1. How else does one explain the lack of organized protest at the manifestly immoral basis of the draft selection procedures of the United States Government (spring 1966)? Incredible though it seems the examination system was designed to separate the efficient members of the community from the less efficient, those in the latter category being conscripted into the armed forces as being, in effect, more expendable to their country. It is a further reflection of the moral obtuseness of our times that a large part of the outcry against these methods of selection, by student groups and other organizations, was directed towards the inefficiency and 'unfairness' of the tests employed – there being allegations that the exam questions favoured the science student as against the art student, the educated against the uneducated, and, therefore, the rich against the poor and the white against the coloured. Employ some 'ideal' test in a thoroughgoing meritocracy and, apparently, such protests would vanish.

as irrelevant happen to be the essential factors in human welfare. An open, easy and full-hearted relationship with one's fellows, for instance, is not something that can be bought, or contrived, or willed into being. The indispensable ingredient of such a relationship is mutual trust, a quality nurtured in the small agrarian society based on mutual dependence, and one of the first casualties in any society whose energies are drawn into the competitive scramble for material ends.

It is undeniably more efficient that infants should imbibe amusement from the television screen rather than that a parent's time and energy be diverted to the telling of bedtime stories. It is incomparably more efficient to turn a knob of a panel in order to capture the music of a celebrated symphony orchestra than to depend upon a solo or duet performance by members of the family or by family friends. The reproduction on a modern record-player of the voice of some great singer is, on an aesthetic plane, likely to be far superior to the sound produced by a man's daughter playing the piano, or the harpsichord. Yet with the passing of these once-common domestic occasions, victims of technological progress, some essential sweetness in the lives of men has also passed away. And it must be said yet again that, although these options are not necessarily closed to us merely because we now have, in addition, gramophones, radios and television sets, their reality is effectively destroyed. Just as in the passing of the independent craftsman, what matters is the altered social significance of these activities in the modern world. The old-time family evening, entertaining each other with song, music or reading, is a pretty thing yet, and in defying the high-powered entertainment world of today, brave even to poignancy. But when the sound of music can flood a room at a flick of a finger, nobody depends any longer for his comfort or cheer upon the affection of his family, the alacrity of his neighbours, or the heartiness of the assembled company. It must be owned that efficiency has triumphed, and the pleasure that once flowed between player and listener in the home, and the singing in which the family would join and warm to each other – these things, in the West, belong to the world we have lost.

The Cult of Efficiency

Passing on to the teaching machines that are currently being developed, it is readily granted that the high hopes placed on them by our most spirited pace-setters will be fulfilled, and that their gradual improvement will enable future generations to be taught more efficiently than students are taught today. As for the university-of-the-air project mooted by our go-ahead politicians, it is all too plausible a vision of the morrow. As surely as efficiency remains the touchstone, it will be realized in the not-too-distant-future. After all, it does not require a particularly bright techno-crat to pose the question: why pay several score lecturers to teach the same subject in different universities in Britain when the growing army of undergraduates, hungry for the 'meal-ticket' and increasingly fearful of not getting the very best, could all simultaneously tune in to some silver-tongued super-lecturer? Televised lectures would be supplemented by auto-instructional programmes in the homes as an efficient and highly economical substitue for conventional tutorials and seminars. Indeed, in view of the existing technological possibilities, it is legitimate to doubt whether the universities as we know them today, as seats of both teaching and learning, will survive the turn of the century.

Yet if people are to be taught more effectively in the future while employing but a fraction of the teaching resources required today, there will also be a loss, the unmeasurable loss of human contact. Just as television has already succeeded in fragmenting the family, and in impoverishing the common fund of mutual experience through which the sense of family is nourished, so also must television apparatus and the teaching machines that are being installed in our universities and our schools serve in time to isolate people further. The youngster of today, seen from the future, is a victim of the wastes of conventional teaching methods and is, consequently, less proficient than the youngster of to-morrow. But today, at least, he is held together in companionship with his classmates – together with them to exult and despair, to groan and to laugh – sharing with them the vital interchanges of sympathy that accompanies their learning through a teacher with, and through whom, whether they mostly love him or hate him, they explore the resources of human feeling.

211

With this crucial factor in mind one may appreciate the acknowledged difficulty of giving impetus in the newly built suburbs and towns to something resembling a community spirit – something that was common enough in yesterday's slums which, for all the dirt and distress, had much in them that was warmly human. A strong sense of community is not a synthetic product to be created *ab initio* by skilful plugging at common interests. The sense of community requires the fact of community, an environment of direct human interdependence. And though scientists and scholars may still be able to share intellectual experiences at some point along the extending frontiers of knowledge, for the common man this prospect does not exist. For him, the doors of communication with his fellows, indeed with his family, are gradually closing as his overt need of them disappears before the relentless advance of an all-embracing technology.

In the older forms of social organization which began to disappear in the early nineteenth century it was just this inescapable fact of close interdependence that held the family and the community together. In the historical circumstances the interdependence was inevitable, yet there was unabashed satisfaction in affirming it. The centripetal forces of modern transport and communications had yet to emerge. In the meantime, in village or town, the lives of the inhabitants were dominated by local events. Narrow though their lives might appear by our megalopolitan standards they had, rich and poor, young and old, their place in the natural order of things, a settled relationship to one another guided by a network of custom and mutual obligation. Inevitably, then, they were, all of them, at the centre of the gossip and the interest, all of them part of the prior and absorbing concern of the community they dwelt in.

III

Generations have passed, and, like the woods and hedges that sheltered it, the rich local life centred on township, parish and village has been uprooted and blown away by the winds of change. Today no refuge remains from the desperate universal clamour for more efficiency, more excitement, and more novelty that goads us furiously onward, competing, accumulating, innovating – and inevitably destroying. Every step forward in technological progress, and particularly in the things most eagerly anticipated – swifter travel, depersonalized services, all the push-button comforts and round-the-clock synthetic entertainment that are promised us – effectively transfers our dependence upon other human beings to dependence upon machines[2] and, therefore, unavoidably constricts yet further the direct flow of understanding and sympathy between people. Thus in the unending pursuit of progress men are driven ever farther apart and come to depend instead, for all their services and experiences, directly upon the creations of technology.

2. Neighbourhoods have degenerated into geographical locations – 'dormitory areas' in which people of like circumstances occupy the houses or blocks of flats along several streets. Each family, nay, each member of each family, has, or soon hopes to have, his own television set and private automobile, the elegant instruments of his estrangement from others. Is it even conceivable for a community to take root in a neighbourhood teeming with cars, transistors and television sets. in which people do not know, or care to know. the names of their neighbours, in which the character of ordinary people, their eccentricities. their spontaneity, their convictions, their once-intimate gossip have all been dried up by the ever-flickering screen? Already we hesitate to call upon friends lest we disturb their television viewings. And, in case we should have nothing better to do than strike up an acquaintance with the adjacent airline-passenger, individual motion-picture entertainment is being installed in order to distract our attention during the whole of the flight.

The era is dawning in which film, television and programmed material will substitute for human teachers; in which the duties of hospital nurses will be taken over by patient-monitoring devices, and medical diagnoses performed by computers. While office staff and skilled workers are being automated into obsolescence, and executives replaced by decision-making machines, game-playing machines are rendering human partners unnecessary. As for sex, for procreative purposes, it is already something of an anachronism. Advances in genetics are about to make fathers expendable; and with the perfection of the mechanical womb, mothers also will become superfluous. We cannot be far from the day of the conversation-machine that will relieve us of obligation to greet politely the occasional recognizable human that strays across our path.

Part Four

13

Concluding Remarks

I

AT the close of our journey it will be useful for the reader to look back over the terrain we have covered and, with the help of some further observations, to pick out the main features.

We began this essay by suggesting that the preoccupation with index economics – the state of our foreign reserves, interest rates, export performance, price movements and other economic events bearing on the 'health' of the economy – leaves us little time to think anew about the social rationale of today's highly developed economies and the goals, if any, they should set themselves. Thus, men in authority, concerned with the day-to-day problems of the economy, have not troubled to re-examine, in the light of new circumstances, the old economic presumptions in favour of competition, free trade, expanding markets and economic growth. There may, however, be some excuse for this persistent concern with what may be called the small change of economics rather than with the fundamental questions. The postwar period has been one of recurring economic crises – or, rather, pseudo-crises, since apart from a propensity to import rather too much[1] there is little that is basically at fault in the British economy. The tendency, over recent years, for imports to outrun exports could, in any case, have easily been avoided had we been less eager to lend abroad or to act as international policemen – or more willing, on occasion, to impose quantitative controls on any of a wide range of relatively expendable imports. Be that as it may, since the

1. Though only if we include in imports current military expenditure and current long-term lending abroad. Indeed, if we ignore the problem of the sterling balances, our balance of payments over the last six years appears to be stronger than that of any of the Common Market countries. Some of the evidence for this belief may be found in an excellent paper by W. A. P. Manser, 'The UK Balance of Payments – A Bar to the European Community?' (*Westminster Bank Review*, November 1966).

additional exports required to balance our excess of imports would take up hardly more than one per cent of our national product – less than the amount by which on the average our national product increases each year – it is arrant nonsense to talk about the drastic efforts we must make in order to 'pay our way in the world'. As for postwar inflation, in Britain at least, it may be attributable in part to rising material expectations explicitly encouraged by successive governments. More important, implicit political constraints – in particular, the apparent commitment to an inflationary level of employment and a pegged exchange rate – have both caused minor crises and then exaggerated their seriousness. There is a marked reluctance in financial and government circles to face the fact that price stability is apparently inconsistent with a 98 per cent level of employment, at least in the absence of near-total controls. There is no less of a reluctance to envisage the possibility of establishing a flexible exchange rate, with the result that whenever our imports tend to exceed our exports, and holders of sterling become jittery, we can react in only one way: push up Bank rate and exert a downward pressure on the economy as a whole, a tortuous and unnecessary process. Frequent and harsh ministerial warnings have the further effect of magnifying the problem out of all economic proportion and have managed to convey the impression, to the public at home and abroad, of a nation tottering into insolvency.

Notwithstanding clumsy policy measures, we may, of course, in time balance our payments, or even generate an export surplus, and, given more time, again return to a condition of import surplus. If, however, we prefer to promote a more stable economic atmosphere, one that will enable us to turn from the fascination of balance-of-payments movements to matters of greater moment, we should be thinking hard about ways of introducing increased flexibility into exchange rates and the money supply. To the extent we succeed we shall be able to leave the balance of payments to look after itself and also, therefore, to formulate domestic policies by reference always to domestic requirements not, as at present, by reference to the gold reserves or to the mood of Zurich bankers.

Turning from matters of 'economic health' to long-term objectives, the essay urges a reconsideration of the place of growth in the economic policy of a technologically advanced society. The notion of economic expansion as a process on balance beneficial to society goes back at least a couple of centuries, about which time, however, the case in favour was much stronger than it is today, when we are not only incomparably wealthier but also suffering from many disagreeable by-products of rapid technological change. Yet so entrenched are the interests involved, commercial, institutional and scientific, and so pervasive the influence of modern communications, that economic growth has embedded itself in the ethos of our civilization. Despite the manifest disamenities caused by the postwar economic expansion, no one today seeking to advance his position in the hierarchy of government or business fails to pay homage to this sovereign concept.

II

The general conclusion of this volume is that the continued pursuit of economic growth by Western societies is more likely on balance to reduce rather than increase social welfare. And some additional light on the pattern of arguments employed is shed by enumerating the set of conditions that, if met, would ensure a positive relation between economic growth and welfare.

First, that the economy be highly competitive in structure in all its branches, or else so organized that in all sectors the outputs of goods are such that their prices tend to equal their corresponding marginal costs.[2]

2. Perhaps it should be repeated that these conditions are sufficient, though *not* necessary. Necessary conditions would be more difficult to specify. The allocative requirements, for instance, if expressed as a necessary condition in conjunction with the others, would state that any given technological advance, or increase in the stock of capital, should not be offset by a worsening of allocation. One cannot be more specific, since there are an unlimited number of ways in which the allocation could be sufficiently worse (in the sense that, notwithstanding technological advance or capital

Second, that all the measurable effects on other people or firms arising in the production and use of any good – other than those effects which already register on the market mechanism in the form of alterations in product and factor prices – be brought into the cost calculus.

Third, that in increasing *per capita* output over time the process of economic growth does not bring about a less equitable distribution of income.

Fourth, that the consuming public be fully conversant with the comparative qualities and performances of all new goods coming on to the market.

Fifth, that the public, regarded as producers, become no worse off in adapting themselves to new techniques of production.

Sixth, that the so-called relative income hypothesis does not hold; or, less stringently, that an overall increase in real income *per capita* will have more than negligible effects in making some people feel better off without making others feel worse off.

Seventh, that the welfare experienced by men from sources other than goods produced by the economic system is small enough to be neglected.

Though it goes without saying that none of these conditions is likely to be met in today's wealthy societies, some of the conditions are more important than others. Observations, both slight and significant, on each of the first six conditions may be found in the professional literature. Since it lends itself to elegant formulation, the first condition is the one treated in most detail. Indeed, owing to the traditional presumption in favour of competition

accumulation, the associated reallocation would be such that it would not be possible to redistribute the new set of outputs as to make everyone better off).

Though of theoretical interest, such difficulties need not detain us here. The choice of statement of any one sufficient condition, rather than another, is only incidental to the main object of drawing attention to the range of considerations that must be attended before one can draw any conclusion about the movement of social welfare.

and free trade, measures of the degree of monopoly in the economy and, occasionally, of allocative waste associated therewith, are of continued interest to economists. Yet the scope for improvements in welfare by policies designed to increase competition is, I should think, very slight in comparison with the losses of welfare from neglect of the other conditions. The concern with external effects, relevant to the second condition, is hardly less pronounced. A good deal of the interest in these external effects, however, may be imputed to the intellectual fascination with optimality problems – not, alas, to universal alarm at what is happening to our environment. I have suggested that the potential contribution to social welfare of adopting a policy of correcting outstanding external diseconomies is vastly underrated, and this for several reasons: (i) because of the present difficulties of measurement; (ii) because of the mistaken view that the disamenities inflicted are limited, since there appear to be incentives to voluntary agreement for their control; and (iii) because of a sense of resignation induced by the slippery problems connected with hypothetical and actual compensation. To these professional reasons we may add the popular impression – which in consequence of the above reasons also appeals to many economists – that economic growth provides a more direct and certain means of advancing welfare.

Most of the space of Part II has been taken up with this question of external diseconomies for the straightforward reason that, more than any of the other matters in the six remaining conditions, an increased public awareness of their nature and logic is the pre-condition to a change in the present order of priorities, one that would enable us to enjoy immediate and substantial social benefits. The current difficulties of measurement are acknowledged. Nevertheless, it is urged that an appreciation of the principles involved helps one to form some idea of the extent of the damage. The concept of amenity rights is invoked in order to provide an equitable basis for actual compensatory payments wherever practicable. Legal support of such rights, moreover, tends to reduce the costs of voluntary agreement for effecting social improvements. Finally, it was pointed out that in many circumstances it is more economic and politically more acceptable to provide separate facilities within any area containing people of unlike views than instead to enforce an optimal arrangement for the area as a whole.

In illustrating some of the chief sources of external diseconomies no attempt was made to disguise the author's conviction that the invention of the private automobile is one of the great disasters to have befallen the human race. Given the absence of controls, the growth of population and its increased wealth and urbanization would, in any case, have produced overgrown cities. Commercial and municipal greed, coupled with architectural apathy, share the responsibility for a litter of shabby buildings. But it needed the motor-car to consummate these developments, to fill our days with clamour and fumes, to suburbanize the countryside and to subtopianize suburbia, and to ensure that any resort which became accessible should simultaneously become unattractive. The motor industry has come to dominate the economy as brazenly as its products dominate our physical environment, and our psychology. The common sight today, of street after street strewn thick with lay-about cars, no longer dismays us.

The other two rapidly growing sources of disamenity used in illustrating the external diseconomies thesis were air-travel and tourism. No effective legislation putting the onus on airlines has been contemplated. The noise created is limited only by what the authorities believe people can be made to put up with. And the public may be conditioned over time to bear with increasing disturbance simply (i) because of the difficulties and cost of organizing protests; (ii) because of the apparent hopelessness of prevailing upon the authorities to put the claims of the residents before the claims of 'progress', that is, the airlines; and (iii) because of the timidity felt in pressing one's claims against so effective a retort as 'the national interest'. If there is a national interest, however, our discussion reveals the case for the government's bearing the cost of its safeguard; not the unfortunate victims of aerial disturbance. The least that should be done to promote social welfare is to extend to the public some choice in the matter by legislating for wholly noise-free zones – zones that are, however, desirable in other respects and easily accessible.

As for the rapid destruction by mass-tourism of the world's dwindling resources of natural beauty, a small contribution towards preservation could be made by the prohibition of motorized vehicles within selected areas and by the discontinuing of air services to such areas. Once the public becomes aware of the spread of devastation, international agreement on more radical measures may be forthcoming – if by then there is anything left worth preserving.

In sum, the thesis of the first two parts of this essay is that if men are concerned primarily with human welfare, and not primarily with productivity conceived as a good in itself, they should reject economic growth as a prior aim of policy in favour of a policy of seeking to apply more selective criteria of welfare. Such a policy would involve (1) legislation recognizing the individual's right to amenity, which legislation would spearhead the attack on much of our postwar blight; and (2) a substantial diversion of investible resources from industry to the task of re-planning our towns and cities – in general, to direct our national resources and our ingenuity to re-creating an environment that will gratify and inspire men. Finally, if public opinion cannot, for the present, be swung overwhelmingly towards this alternative view of the primary ends of policy, any regard at all to the declared doctrine of increasing the range of choices available to men warrants an extension to existing minorities of separate facilities in matters both large and small – though especially in respect of viable areas wherein a man of moderate means may choose to dwell unmolested by those particular features of modern technology that most disturb his equanimity.

III

If the moving spirit behind economic growth were to speak, its motto would be 'Enough does not suffice'. The classical description of an economic system makes sense in today's advanced economy only when stood on its head. Certainly the American economy presents us with a spectacle of growing resources pressing against limited wants. Moreover the pace of change in the patterns of people's wants destroys the base on which the economist's comparison of social welfare is raised: if all seven conditions mentioned were met, the mere fact of continually changing tastes alone would prevent the economist from inferring that economic growth *per capita* increased welfare. Moreover, the vagaries of fashion can become burdensome and the multiplication of goods disconcerting.

Once we move away from the economist's frame of reference, other factors bearing on social welfare loom large. Expanding markets in conditions of material abundance depend upon men's dissatisfaction with their lot being perpetually renewed. Whether individual campaigns are successful or not, the institution of commercial advertising accentuates the materialistic tendencies in society and promotes the view that the things that matter most are the things money will buy – a view to which the young, who have plenty of need of the wherewithal, if they are to avail themselves of the widely advertised opportunities for fast living and cool extravagance, are peculiarly vulnerable, and which explains much of their vociferous impatience and increasing violence.

These and other informal considerations brought to bear in the digression of Part III lead to pessimistic conclusions. Technological innovations may offer to add to men's material opportunities. But by increasing the risks of their obsolescence it adds also to their anxiety. Swifter means of communication have the paradoxical effect of isolating people; increased mobility has led to more hours commuting; increased automobilization to increased separation; more television to less communication. In consequence, people know less of their neighbours than ever before in history.

The pursuit of efficiency, itself regarded as the lifeblood of progress, is directed towards reducing the dependence of people on each other, and increasing their dependence on the machine. Indeed, by a gradual displacement of human effort from every aspect of living, technology will eventually enable us to slip swiftly through our allotted years with scarce enough sense of physical friction to be certain we are still alive.[3]

Considerations such as these, which do not lend themselves to formal treatment, are crucial to the issue of human welfare. And the apparent inevitability of technological advance does not thereby render them irrelevant. Death too is inevitable. But one does not feel compelled to hurry towards it on that account. Once we descry the the sort of world towards which technological growth is bearing us, it is well worth discussing whether humanity will find it more congenial or not. If, on reflection, we view the prospects with misgivings we are, at least, freed from the obligation to join in the frequent incantations of our patriotic growthmen. More positively, we have an additional incentive to support the policy of reducing industrial investment in favour of large-scale replanning of our cities, and of restoring and enhancing the beauty of many of our villages, towns and resorts.

3. The recent electric-power breakdown in New York (1965), obviously to be deplored on grounds of efficiency, broke the spell of monotony for millions of New Yorkers. People enjoyed the shock of being thrown back on their innate resources and into sudden dependence upon one another. For a few hours people were freed from routine and brought together by the dark. Next-door strangers spoke, and gladdened to help each other. There was room for kindness.

The fault was repaired. The genie of power was returned to each home. And as the darkness brought them stumbling into each other's arms, so the hard light scattered them again. Yet someone was quoted as saying, 'This should happen at least once a month.'

APPENDIX A

Technological Unemployment

OWING to careless exposition in some elementary textbooks the casual student of economics is frequently left with the impression that technological innovation cannot lead to unemployment – the unfortunate Luddites, imagining themselves displaced by machinery, being the victims of vulgar error rather than historical circumstances. In extenuation of this belief in the impossibility of technological unemployment it must be conceded that until not so long ago the dominant view was, and had been for over a century, that neither could unemployment arise from a deficiency of total demand. For with the great equilibrium systems of the Classical economists in mind, it was not easy to envisage underemployment *equilibrium*.

The existence of involuntary unemployment, it was believed, exerted a downward pressure on money wages. And if wages were in the process of decline the position, by definition, could not be one of equilibrium. Moreover, the gradual decline in money wages, it was argued, tended to restore full employment, since any reduction in money wages implied a corresponding reduction in the price level and, through the operation (1) of the cash-balance effect in reducing interest rates that were imperfectly stabilized by speculative activity; and (2) of the asset-expenditure effect in reducing the real volume of saving, the level of employment would rise until all underemployment-pressure on prices ceased. The conclusion that involuntary unemployment could exist only in the short run did not, however, satisfy Keynes, simply because the time required for market forces effectively to reduce such unemployment might be many years. The long-run solution was therefore irrelevant: 'In the long run we are all dead!' The practical thing was for the government to intervene immediately in stimulating effective demand by the several means open to it.

There is something of this older complacency in the popular fallacy that technological unemployment cannot exist. Thus (even if we ignore production functions with regions of negative marginal returns to the abundant factor) a labour-saving innovation may well be such that the existing supply of labour in the economy could be employed only at a real wage materially below that in existence. In a competitive economy in which wages were completely flexible the new technique and the new wage would come to prevail, and anyone who attempted to continue with the old technique would (paying the new wage and rentals) cost himself out of the market. Again, therefore, in some 'long run', full employment would be restored at this lower absolute wage. But if, for institutional reasons, there were determined attempts to maintain the real wage at its pre-automation level, technological unemployment could continue for many years.

Even this argument, however, concedes too much, for two reasons: (1) because with the new methods of production, factor substitution may be negligible. True, there may be several alternative ways of producing a set of goods, but if they are all highly labour-saving then unemployment with zero wages, as the market solution, is consistent with each method – at least, such a solution would prevail in a market with completely flexible factor prices. However, if institutional forces could determine wages and rentals, unemployed labour would continue to exist until capital accumulation reduced the labour–capital ratio to the point at which the existing supply of labour could be employed again at positive wages. A possibly 'academic' solution for highly labour-saving innovations might be to reduce drastically the hours put in by each labourer, though such a solution might well act to reduce technical efficiency.

The other reason (2) is that the assumption of homogeneous labour is too abstract a concept for the relevant economic models. In automation, complex capital equipment is combined with skilled 'brain labour' both in the producing and the operating of the machinery: the whole idea is to dispense not only with unskilled labour but also with highly skilled manual labour and clerical labour. Thus, the proportion of such labour required in any automated process must be expected to decline with the evolution of technology.

Again, it is open to people to be complacent and talk of a long-run 'transformation' of old-type manual labour into new-type brain labour – though even here, since substitutability is likely to be small, it may be a long time before there were sufficient capital to employ the transformed supply of labour. However, it is far from being impossible that in the not-too-distant future a large proportion of the adult population would be *unemployable* simply because they would not be endowed with the innate capacities necessary to acquire the highly developed mental skills which may be called for by a more complex technology. Of course, they may all be comfortably maintained by some transfer of the increased output produced by the reduced working population. There need be no economic crisis, only a social one.

Reduction of Imports *versus*
Expansion of Exports

ON the assumption that we can ignore the political difficulties associated with the alternative methods of meeting an adverse current balance of payments, simple economic analysis brings out sharply the advantages of (*a*) reducing the excess imports directly, either by tariffs or by quantitative restrictions, as compared with (*b*) expanding exports through a reduction of our export prices relative to foreign prices.

(*a*) Let ε_H be the UK's overall price elasticity of demand for foreign goods, which goods, we shall suppose, are produced at constant costs. Since ε_H is defined as $\triangle M/M \div \triangle P/P$, if M is an index of that volume of our imports equal in value to our existing exports, $\triangle M$ an index of our excess imports, and P an index of our import prices, then $\triangle P$ represents the rise in the index of import prices necessary to eliminate $\triangle M$.

Thus, the proportional rise in import prices

$$\triangle P/P = \triangle M/M \cdot 1/\varepsilon_H.$$

An estimate of the loss of consumers' surplus resulting from the rise in import prices, $M \cdot \triangle P + \frac{1}{2} \triangle M \cdot \triangle P$, is more than the loss of net social surplus by the transfer to the government of $M \cdot \triangle P$ (assuming that, in the case of quantitative restrictions, the government sells or auctions the licences necessary to purchase the restricted imports). The net loss of social surplus is, therefore, $\frac{1}{2} \triangle P \triangle M$, or $\frac{1}{2} \triangle P/P (\triangle M \cdot P)$.

In order to convey an idea of the magnitudes involved, suppose our exports were running at the rate of £6 billion per annum and our imports exceeded our exports by £$\frac{1}{2}$billion. Then:

for an ε_H of —1, the required $\triangle P/P \doteqdot 8\frac{1}{2}\%$, and the loss of
social surplus $\doteqdot$ £20m.

for an ε_H of —2, the required $\triangle P/P \doteq 4\%$, and the loss of
social surplus $= £10$m.

for an ε_H of —4, the required $\triangle P/P \doteq 2\%$, and the loss of
social surplus $= £5$m.

(*b*) Turning from the loss incurred in achieving balance by a direct reduction of the excess £½ billion imports to the loss incurred in expanding exports by £½ billion, let E^F be the overall elasticity of foreign *payments* for our exports with respect to their average price, $\triangle(XP)/XP \div \triangle P/P$, where X is the volume index of our exports and P their price index. If $\triangle(XP)$ is the required expansion in the *value* of our exports, the necessary proportional fall in their price index, $\triangle P/P = \triangle(XP)/XP \cdot 1/E_F$, or $\triangle(XP)/XP \cdot 1/(\varepsilon_F+1)$, where ε_F is the overall price elasticity of foreign demand for our exports.

An estimate of the loss sustained by the UK economy on the pre-existing volume of exports, X, is $\triangle P \cdot Z \equiv \triangle P/P \cdot (PX) = \triangle(PX)/\varepsilon_F+1$.

Some notion of the loss entailed by reducing export prices by the amount necessary to expand our export receipts by £½billion, when current exports are £6 billion, is conveyed by the following calculations:

for an ε_F of —1, or above, no price reduction will suffice

for an ε_F of —2, required $\triangle P/P = 8\frac{1}{2}\%$, involving a loss of about £½b.

for an ε_F of —4, required $\triangle P/P = 2\cdot8\%$ involving a loss of about £160m.

The fact that many products enter into the composition of our trade and that the elasticities of demands for the various goods vary with the amounts bought does not of itself suggest any bias in the above illustration. If anything, the advantage of using import controls rather than export expansion may be greater than that suggested by the hypothetical figures. For the imports to be eliminated are likely to be 'luxury' goods, close substitutes with domestic goods, or otherwise expendable amounts of imports having a high elasticity of demand.

A reduction in the excess volume of our imports has the further advantage of being less inflationary than an increase in our exports. This, again, is simple to illustrate if we disregard some obvious refinements. Again we assume current exports to be £6 billion with excess imports of £$\frac{1}{2}$ billion and suppose also a net national income of £25 billion.

(a^1) On the assumption that excess imports of £$\frac{1}{2}$ billion are reduced by tariffs or quantitative restrictions (with licences to import the restricted quantities sold or auctioned by the government), the rise in the price of imports times the quantity imported represents a transfer of purchasing power from the public to the government. If we continue to assume that the government spends the proceeds in much the same way as the public, no alteration in aggregate demand takes place from this facet of the operation. The reduction in the volume of foreign purchases, however, causes the public to switch their purchasing power to domestic goods and, therefore, entails an addition to aggregate domestic demand equal to £$\frac{1}{2}$ billion (or about 2 per cent of national income).

This inflationary impact, presumably met by some measure of anti-inflationary policy, has to be compared with that resulting from the required increase in the volume of our imports.

(b^1) A reduction in the price of our exports does not add to aggregate domestic demand. But the increase in the volume of our exports times the new price does add $\triangle X \cdot P$ to aggregate domestic demand.

Since $\varepsilon_F = \triangle X \cdot P / \triangle P \cdot X$, $\triangle X \cdot P = \varepsilon_F \triangle P \cdot X \equiv \varepsilon_F \triangle P / P \cdot (XP)$. Thus:

for an ε_F of —1, $\triangle P/P$ is infinite.

for an ε_F of —2, $\triangle P/P = 8\frac{1}{2}\%$, and net addition to aggregate domestic demand = £1b. (or 4% of national income).

for an ε_F of —4, $\triangle P/P = 4\%$, and net addition to aggregate domestic demand = £·66b. (or about 2·7% of national income).

Perhaps quantitative restrictions are to be preferred as being more certain in their effects on imports than tariffs (and also, if we do, for a moment, consider the international political aspects, because G A T T frowns on tariffs but permits temporary quantitative restrictions in times of balance-of-payments emergency). Obviously there are other considerations worth discussing in connexion with these alternative methods of restoring balance, but the implications brought out above need to be emphasized.

APPENDIX C

A Note on the Interpretation of the Benefits of Private Transport

I

In this note I construct a hypothetical situation to reveal some of the circumstances under which consumers' surplus, when used as an index of the benefits to be derived from private automobile travel, may give perverse results – a rise in the index being accompanied by a reduction in the benefit experienced by motorists. Less surprisingly it will also be shown that the use of consumers' surplus in determining optimal traffic flows, in benefit-cost studies, and in estimating rates of return in road investment, results in over-investment solutions in road construction unless the alternatives to private automobile travel are properly priced.

Although not essential it will simplify the analysis to assume (1) that in all sections of a fully-employed economy, except those under examination, price is already equal to social marginal cost, and (2), provisionally at least, that there are no neighbourhood effects external to the transport industry that affect the amenity of the public. We can circumvent the appropriate-rate-of-discount problem by estimating the consumers' surplus for each individual in terms of present discounted value of expected surpluses over the future. A measure of this consumer's surplus, based on the Compensating Variation, on the purchase of a new automobile requires the individual to anticipate, at the time of purchase, the total number of miles for which the car will be used, valuing each mile at its maximum present worth to him (net of all variable costs, including fuel and maintenance) and arranging them in descending order to the point of zero maximum worth. This arrangement produces a function $V(m)$ of total expected mileage. After completing M miles the car is to be sold for a sum having a present value of £T. If the car when bought costs £B, including tax,[1] the present discounted value of the compensating-variation

1. This tax may be an underestimate or overestimate of the costs incurred

measure of consumer's surplus, CS, is equal to $_0F^mV(m)dm-(B-T)$, this sum being the maximum the individual would be prepared to pay in order to secure a permit to buy the car at the price £B, given his expectation of re-selling for the sum mentioned after motoring M miles.

Phase I of the situation is one in which there is no private traffic, an efficient system of public transport, say a bus service, linking together all parts of the city. Individual A, typical of others, uses the bus daily to take him to the centre of the city in about ten minutes. Public transport is also used for his occasional outings.

Phase II is the transitional one in which A buys a new car that, in the circumstances prevailing (which he, short-sightedly, projects into the future), is expected to take him to the centre in five minutes. On his anticipations of the future he makes a CS of, say £800. Provided that only A buys a car, and nothing else changes, A is to that extent better off in Phase II than in Phase I.

Phase III occurs after a large enough number of others follow A's example. Within two or three years, we may suppose, the increase in the number of private cars is such that it takes A fifteen minutes to drive to work. He realizes now that he was better off in Phase I, but this opportunity is now closed to him; for owing to the build-up of private traffic the congestion is such that it would take him twenty-five minutes to reach his office by bus. Moreover, since bus drivers have had to be compensated for the increased difficulties and risk of driving, the bus fare has risen.

Phase III′ is the situation which exists when public transport has been withdrawn altogether, as may happen if commercial considerations alone prevail. Analytically, however, it differs from III only in being a more extreme case of it.

II

By assumption A is now worse off in Phase III than he was in I. He would, of course, prefer II to either III or I. But II is a

---

by the community (exclusive of the costs of mutual congestion) in keeping the existing traffic moving on the existing system of roads. The analysis assumes that the tax is exactly equal to the costs incurred.

transitional phase only: it is no longer open to him, and could be reserved for him only if he exercised the powers of a dictator.

Since A is typical of other individuals who have changed from being passengers to being motorists, we can assume that I is *socially* preferred to III. Dealers in motor-cars and accessories may, themselves, be on balance better off, but we suppose that they could not compensate the rest of the community and remain as well off as they were in I.

There are two things to notice: first, that under existing institutions there are no self-generating forces that can restore to the community the socially preferred Phase I. Only a collective decision could return the community from the existing III or III′ phase to the original I situation. Second, that A's CS on his automobile in Phase III will exceed that in Phase II, notwithstanding that he gets less benefit from his automobile in Phase III. It was, in fact, just because public transport was so cheap and efficient in Phase I that the maximum amount he was prepared to pay for successive miles of private driving was lower that it was in Phase III, where the public transport alternative was unattractive. If now, for example, we move to Phase III′, in which the public transport alternative is completely withdrawn, a loss of welfare will certainly be experienced by the remaining passengers. Some of these ex-passengers will have little choice but to purchase automobiles. Compared with their new alternatives, of either walking to work or not working in the city, the CS on their purchases will be positive, and may even be large. Since we may assume that the cars used by the displaced passengers in Phase III′ take up more road space than did the displaced buses, the motorists in Phase III′, of which A was a typical member, will also be worse off than they were in III.

If the benefit conferred by the private automobile on its owner is measured by his CS, or any proxy measure, the chronological change through II, III and III′ will appear to register a continuously increasing benefit notwithstanding the continuous deterioration in his welfare in this respect.

A similar development could of course arise in other situations, for instance in a suburb linked by rail to the city. At the given rail fare, n commuters are required in order for the railway to 'break even'. If, therefore, owing to an initial change from rail to road, only m commuters remain ($m < n$), the railway service must close down. The closure clearly makes the m commuters worse off. But it also makes those who were, before the closure, travelling by private automobile worse off, (a) because m commuters now have to travel by road and increase the congestion there; and (b) because even though automobile travellers made no use of the railway, or used it infrequently, it did provide a form of insurance in the case of the car being out of service – or for such occasions when, for one reason or another, the motorist did not feel up to driving.

Again, however, despite the fact that everyone going into the city is adversely affected by the railway closure, the community's demand for road travel will be seen to have expanded and the individual and, therefore, the collective consumers' surplus of automobile owners will reveal a gain. Each ex train-commuter who has now perforce to purchase an automobile must reveal a positive C S. As for the remainder, once the railway service has been removed the only alternative, we may suppose, is walking to the city. The maximum amount any individual would be willing to pay for the ith journey by car is consequently greater.

III

These simple illustrations may serve to remind the transport expert that there are difficulties other than those of statistical measurement. Not only can the index of consumers' benefit rise over time without any actual experience of benefit – simply because 'real' income is increasing, and therefore people are prepared to pay more for the ith unit of any good, or service, whose actual utility to them in fact remains unchanged – but such an index can rise concurrently with an actual reduction of benefit. The more significant parts of the *ceteris paribus* of all consumer's surplus (and rent) analysis relate to the constancy of the prices, and/or availabilities of, the close substitutes, and complements, for the good or service in question. The more effective the good y

as, say, a substitute for x, the smaller will be the consumer's surplus on purchases of x at the given prices. Raise the price of y, and ultimately withdraw it from the market, and this simultaneously reduces the welfare of the consumer and increases his measure of consumer's surplus on purchases of x.

The same illustrations also serve to show that any allocative recommendations flowing from such estimates of the demand curve for automobile travel are invalid in the absence of optimal outputs in the alternative services. In the first illustration, as the community moves into Phase III the transport expert may continue to revise upward his estimate of the 'optimal traffic flow',[2] which expands, therefore, along with the fall in motorists' welfare. Of course, in the event of Phase III' being reached, there remaining no alternative but to walk to work, the elasticity of demand may be so low as to make little difference, if any, between the actual traffic flow and the optimal traffic flow.

The transport expert may also use the data in III and III' to justify investment in road-widening, in fly-overs, freeways, and bridges, in the attempt to accommodate the expanding number of private automobiles.

Now if there were effective methods for imputing congestion costs in the first place, other recommendations would follow which, under our assumption that in all other sectors price was equal to social marginal cost, could be justified. Beginning with a satisfactory public transport in Phase I, such a mechanism would require that full compensation for any inconvenience caused to every passenger and bus driver by the marginal car be imputed to the marginal car. Such a scheme would ensure that no additional car be allowed on the route(s) in question unless it were able to effect a Pareto improvement – the owner of the car being at least no worse off after compensating everyone else using the roads –

2. By calculating the marginal congestion cost of traffic $dC/D = dC/dT \cdot dT/dS \cdot dS/dN$, where C is total congestion cost, N the number of vehicles, T the total time taken by the traffic over the given route ($=tN$ where t is the average time taken per automobile) and S is the average speed of traffic over that route. The optimal traffic flow is that which equates marginal congestion costs $\frac{dC}{dN}$ to the demand price $P(N)$ for that route.

bus passengers, bus drivers, and intra-marginal automobiles. Such a requirement, which would ensure growing benefits from traffic, might well entail an optimal flow with very few private automobiles.

Be that as it may, it is only *after* this optimal flow is established that one may proceed correctly to estimate the returns to investment in road-widening, freeways and other traffic-accommodating projects. A traffic flow that has not been corrected implies that marginal congestion costs exceed marginal benefit for some part of the existing traffic flow. Total congestion costs incurred being, then, so much greater than the optimally determined congestion costs, the saving by traffic investment will appear correspondingly greater. It is possible, therefore, that an initial optimal traffic flow might reveal no economic case for traffic investment, whereas failure to establish this optimal flow would allow traffic to pile up congestion costs and would therefore enable investment to appear profitable in effect by reducing excess traffic costs that were not warranted in the first place.

Similar remarks apply to our second illustration. If as a consequence of rail closure congestion occurs on the road connecting the suburb to the city, the establishment of an optimal flow of motorized traffic must precede any estimate of the benefits of road investment. More important, the rationale of the proposed rail closure itself should be scrutinized before this requirement. A fall in the number of fare-paying passengers below some critical number *n* is generally irrelevant in this connexion. The line should be kept running for the time being, if, at any number of passengers for which price is equal to marginal operating costs, total benefit exceeds total operating costs.[3] Benefits may be reckoned as the sum of three items: (*a*) the fares that could be collected of all those willing to pay the marginal cost price (as determined by the existing demand schedule) plus the consumer's surplus of every such individual; (*b*) the insurance value of the railway service to those who do not anticipate any particular railway journeys; and (*c*) the sum total of any (additional) congestion costs

3. Largely the earnings of *necessary* personnel, fuel and maintenance charges.

that would be inflicted on all motorists having to use the suburb-to-city road after the railway closure.[4] It would not be surprising if many of the railway services closed or due for closure could prove economic viability by meeting these conditions. At all events, closing a railway service that, on this criterion, ought not to be closed entails a misallocation of shiftable resources currently being used by the railway. Having misallocated resources by closing down the railway service, investment in roads that would otherwise (if the railway service were available) be clearly seen as wasteful might well appear profitable.

IV

We have confined ourselves in this note to external diseconomies that are internal to private motoring, i.e. to the mutual congestion costs of motorized traffic, following the popular custom of relegating to a parenthetical remark the unmeasurable, though probably much more important, effects on the physical environment. The private car carries along with it, however, a much neglected disamenity-potential through its being the chief agent of rapid urban sprawl and ribbon building. As 'developers' set up estates farther and yet farther from city centres, in the assurance that wherever they site their buildings families with private cars will be prepared to make the longer journey in order to live in country areas, the advantages of those families already settled in these areas are diminished.[5]

Even if we restrict the analysis to a given area, say the city and

4. To be more exact (c) should be included in so far as this contingent addition to congestion has not been anticipated. If it were wholly anticipated, it would have raised the consumer's surpluses of existing and potential railway users, and would have raised the value of the railway to motorists who make no regular use of the railway.

5. Again, however, if some institutional mechanism could be established whereby each additional home-buyer (who adds to the existing number in or near the area and so contributes to its transformation into a suburb) were obliged to compensate existing householders for the loss of amenity endured by his settling there, the criterion for a Pareto improvement could be met. Such external diseconomies would then be automatically corrected and urban sprawl be subject to a built-in check.

its dormitory areas, the continual visual disturbance, the pollution of the air by exhaust fumes, the incessant engine noise and vibration generated by any *n* travellers using private transport are very many times those generated by the same number using public transport instead, in particular if public transport were electrically powered. Hence, although an optimal flow of traffic calculated with respect only to mutual traffic frustration already favours public transport at the expense of private transport (comparing this optimal flow with the usual free-for-all that makes road investment appear so profitable; an optimal flow that also takes into consideration these other environment-damaging consequences – no less relevant or significant for being statistically elusive – would further reduce the warrantable flow of private traffic. If the number of private-car journeys consistent with this more comprehensive measure of the optimal flow were believed to be few, the costs involved in their regulation might well suggest the prohibition within a given area of all private traffic as the most economic solution – allowing, perhaps, for a given number of private taxis within the area for emergency purposes.

It may well happen that, contrary to our initial assumption, the existing public transport was inadequate in the first place with respect to coverage, speed and frequency. However, an analysis that yields a Pareto optimal solution requiring the provision of an efficient public transport service does not depend upon the chronological sequence posited for its validity.[6]

6. In general, if each vehicle differed in size and other relevant characteristics, and if the value attached by the occupants of each vehicle to travelling the distance in question differed for any i^{th} journey, we should determine the optimal traffic flow and its composition by maximizing the social surplus. This is got by ranking the individual journeys by the excess of CV over the marginal congestion cost until the excess is zero. In the absence of welfare effects on the CV measure, which would be brought into operation by compensatory payments, the optimal flow and composition of the traffic is uniquely determined. For any flow having a social surplus smaller than this maximum indicates a potential Pareto improvement. Thus some journey(s) currently excluded by the composition of the existing traffic could replace some journey(s) currently included, and thereby increase the social surplus. The additional gain from such exchange operations could, of course, be distributed among the participants as to make each of them better off.